Once upon a Word

True Tales of Word Origins
Rob Kyff

Tapestry Press
Irving, Texas

Tapestry Press
3649 Conflans Road
Suite 103
Irving, TX 75061

Printed in the U.S.A.
07 06 05 04 03 1 2 3 4 5

Library of Congress Cataloging-in-Publication Data
Kyff, Rob, 1948-
Once upon a word : true tales of word origins / by Rob Kyff.
    p. cm.
Includes index.
ISBN 1-930819-29-3 (trade paper : alk. paper)
1. English language--Etymology. I. Title.
PE1574.K94 2003
422--dc21

                              2003007036

Cover and book design and layout by
D. & F. Scott Publishing, Inc.
N. Richland Hills, Texas

This book is dedicated to
Christopher Cypher (1948–2001), cherished friend,
and
Lisa Ellen Kyff (1953–2001), beloved sister

Contents

Foreword

To the man or woman who knows its origin, each word presents a picture, no matter how ordinary it may appear. Sometimes, time has so ravaged the images that no trace is left. In most instances, surface grime can be wiped away, restoring the beauty of the contours, colors, and details.

Word pictures are like family snapshots. Discovering the origin of a word or phrase gives us the same pleasure we experience when our grandparents or parents open up the family album and tell us stories about the people gazing out from the pages. Hearing tales about those who came before us and uncovering those odd, buried, Old World family mysteries helps us to learn whence we came and who we are.

The poet William Cowper once wrote of

> *philologists who trace*
> *A panting syllable through time and space,*
> *Start it at home, and hunt it in the dark*
> *To Gaul, to Greece, and into Noah's ark.*

Rob Kyff is an expert wordhunter-gatherer. He loves stalking words back through early modern history, through classical times, yea, back even to Noah. Rob Kyff knows that words are our forebears, that most were born long before we were and bequeath us their rich legacies. In illuminating the faded pictures of time-hallowed words and phrases, *Once upon a Word* shines light on our history and our customs, our working and our playing, our loving and our fighting, and our praying and our sinning.

Richard Lederer
San Diego, California

Acknowledgments

The word *friend* comes from the German root *fri-*, which means to love, like, be friendly to. That derivation doesn't surprise me, for my friends have loved, liked and been friendly to me throughout my life, and especially during the writing of this book.

I'm especially grateful to Tim Armour, Lud Baldwin, Frank Beatty, David Brooks, Paul Burton, Dick Caley, Chris Carlson, Rich Chiarappa, Jerry Chichester, Molly Cooper, Bob Del Torto, Joe Duffy, Wally Goldstein, Bob Googins, John Horan, Bill Hunt, Dave Mellen, Ted Levine, Brock Putnam, Larry Roberts, Dick Sheehan, John Sherfinski, Jim Skiff, Joe Strayhorn, John Strother and Joan Walden. And I owe a special debt of gratitude to my sister and most faithful fan, Pamela Kyff.

My colleagues in the Trout Brook Writers Group—Jim Cahalan, Laura Hansen, Alex Kraus, Gary Pandolfi, Pat Rosoff and Ann Serow—sustained and encouraged me as I began my writing career. Two heads of school at Kingswood-Oxford School—Tyler Tingley and Lee Levison—have not only allowed me to reduce my teaching load to allow time for my writing but also supported me personally and professionally.

A writer is only as good as his editors, and mine have been gentle and patient shepherds of my often wayward talent. I'm especially grateful to Kyrie O'Connor and Joe Nunes, who edit my column "Word Watch" for the *Hartford Courant*, and to Katherine Searcy, who edits my column "The Word Guy" for Creators Syndicate.

Jill Bertolet of Tapestry Press has not only believed in this book from beginning but has also boosted, bolstered, and buoyed me through every step of the publication process. The talent and professionalism of Jill and her associates, as well as their friendliness and warmth, have made the publication process both rewarding and enjoyable.

My literary agent, Jim Cypher, has been my mentor, sounding board, and number-one cheerleader. He saw the potential in this project when it was still a collection of untold tales, and he worked patiently and persistently to make it happen, even when my own hope and energy flagged.

Finally, I want to thank both my teachers and my students. Their keen curiosity and intellectual passion have invigorated my own sense of wonder. They are the true authors of this book.

Introduction

When we first meet a person, we want to know not only where that person lives and what he does, but also where he comes from—his hometown, family background, education.

We share the same curiosity about the origins of words. Why, for instance, is an old building said to be *dilapidated*? Where does the word *scandal* come from? Why is a blonde a *towhead*? Why is a second-rate adventure novel called a *pot boiler*? Why do we *bone up* on a subject? Why do people who improvise *wing it*?

Discovering the origin of a word or phrase can breathe new life into that term for us. As St. Isadore of Seville observed way back in the seventh century, "When you see whence a name has arisen, you will understand its force." Learning, for instance, that *dilapidated* once referred to walls with missing stones imparts a new appreciation for the tumble-down feel of this word. And when we realize that *scandal* once denoted a trap, we have a bit more sympathy for a Hollywood starlet ensnared by the tabloids.

Some words have double and even triple incarnations. Blondes are called *towheads*, for instance, because their hair resembles yellow flax (called *tow*) prepared for spinning. In turn, nineteenth-century steamboat captains called yellow sandbars *towheads* because they looked like blond heads poking above the river.

Just as a person's initial appearance can deceive or mislead us, so can words. You might guess, for instance, that thrill-a-minute adventure stories are labeled *potboilers* because they keep their plots bubbling along. In fact, they're so called because impoverished authors often write popular fiction just to make money for food, to keep their own stew pots boiling,

Or we might assume that *bone up* has something to do with working ourselves to the bone to learn something; in fact, it comes from the Bohn publishing company, which printed handy translations of Latin and Greek works for students. Likewise, to *wing it* refers, not to flying, but to theater, where unprepared actors are fed their lines by prompters standing in the wings.

But there's an even more delicious reason to uncover the stories behind words: sheer delight. "Even the deadest word," Ralph Waldo Emerson noted, was "once a brilliant picture." And most of these brilliant pictures are amusing, charming, and amazing.

A surprising number of words and phrases, for instance, are based on human duplicity. *Shoddy* originally referred to a woolen fabric so inferior that Civil War uniforms made from it fell apart in the rain. *Gerrymander* evolved when Elbridge Gerry redrew a Congressional district so outrageously and grotesquely that it resembled a salamander. And *credenza* derives from the Latin word for trust. In royal courts, no food was placed on a certain table without first being tested by the royal taster; so a king knew this meal—and the piece of furniture it sat on—could be trusted.

Other words evolved through oddball chains of events involving human error, misunderstanding or coincidence. Through some mysterious process, for instance, *husband*, which originally meant the *mistress* of a house, came to mean the *master* of a house. Similarly, for no apparent reason, someone added an *r* to the Old English *bryd-guma* to create *bridegroom*. People mispronounced *bitts end* (the end of a ship's anchor chain) so often that it became *bitter end*. And the British compressed the pronunciations of *Mary Magdalene* and *St. Audrey* into near unintelligibility, but in the process gave us the new words *maudlin* and *tawdry*, respectively.

So, as you open this book, imagine yourself entering a roomful of intriguing new people. As they introduce themselves, you'll meet many fascinating characters—each with a unique and wondrous tale to tell.

BODY LANGUAGE

Hip Terms and Knee-ologisms

The English language is a notorious body snatcher. From *heads up* to *toe the line*, it has stolen hundreds of words and phrases from the human anatomy. It's no surprise that the human body has provided a "handy" source of words and phrases for the English language.

Bone Appetit!

Here's your chance to bone up on some bone-a fide English expressions.

make no bones about it—During the Middle Ages, an era when the good that men did was oft interred with their bones, the stews they dined on were oft filled with small bones. If you were lucky enough to find no bones in your stew, you had nothing to stew about, so the expressions *find no bones* and *make no bones* came to mean have no difficulty or hesitation. Among Mafia dons, to *make your bones* means to perform a criminal act, such as murder, to demonstrate your loyalty to the crime family. Some have linked this term to the murder victim's bones, but this isn't regarded as a *bona fide* explanation.

bone up—Those who say *bone up* refers to studying so hard that the material becomes part of your bones are merely engaging in linguistic skullduggery. And those who say it refers to making your knowledge stronger, the way whalebone once *boned up* corsets, are just ribbing us. In fact, *bone up* isn't bred in the *bone* at all. It's derived from the Bohn Publishing Co., which, between 1860 and 1910, printed transla-

1

tions of Latin and Greek works. Students who relied on these books were said to *Bohn up* on their homework.

bonfire—Bid *bon voyage* to the notion that *bonfire* comes from the French *bon* (good) and the Anglo-Saxon *fire*. The *bon* in *bonfire* is made of bone. During the Middle Ages, people lit *bone fyres* fueled by bones of sheep, oxen and other animals to celebrate midsummer holy days such as the eves of St. John and St. Peter. Later, any celebratory conflagration, whether it consumed wood, leaves, books or even an occasional hapless heretic, was called a *bonfire*. So the derivation of *bonfire* is not bonny, but bony. Oh, well. Here today, gone to marrow.

Neck-rophilia

For a relatively small part of the body, the neck has given us a surprisingly large number of colorful terms. Let's do some linguistic rubbernecking.

neck of the woods—One meaning of the Old English word *hnecca*, which gave us our modern word *neck*, was a narrow stretch of land. This meaning survives in several place names in the Northeast, e.g., Great Neck on Long Island, Haddam Neck in Connecticut, and Horse Neck Beach in Rhode Island. But the expression *neck of the woods* originated in America, not Great Britain. Linguist Bill Bryson suggests it may have been derived from the Algonquin Indian word *naiack*, meaning point or corner.

red neck—Etymologists have grown red in the face, if not the neck, debating the origins of this term. According to the *Oxford English Dictionary*, *redneck* was first used in 1830 to describe a group of Presbyterians in Fayetteville, North Carolina. Later it came to mean the rural poor of the South and eventually any person perceived as narrow-minded or bigoted. Some attribute the red necks of rural Southerners to the effects of the disease pellagra, others to sunburn acquired while working in the fields, but I prefer a dirtier explanation: The soil in much of Dixie is red, so when perspiring Southern farmers rubbed the backs of their necks, their necks became red.

rubberneck—According to Irving Lewis Allen's book *The City in Slang*, this term evolved in New York City during the 1890s to describe gawking tourists who craned and stretched their necks to see points of interest from sightseeing wagons or buses. Linguist H. L. Mencken loved the term *rubberneck*, calling it "one of the best words ever coined" and "almost a complete treatise on American psychology." Whoever invented it, he wrote, should receive "half a bushel of medals."

necking—As long as we're giving out bushels of medals, perhaps the person who invented *necking* should receive a bushel—and a peck. *Necking* was first used by the "flaming youth" of the 1920s to mean kiss and caress amorously. Mencken apparently liked this Americanism too; in 1926, his *American Mercury* magazine noted that some people opposed "theater, dancing, necking."

bottleneck—It's easy to see how a narrow point where traffic jammed up came to be compared to a neck of a bottle. What's surprising is that it took people so long to do it. This term wasn't invented until the early 1900s, presumably as a response to the increasing congestion in crowded cities. Some linguists have cited the illogic of the commonly used phrases "huge bottleneck" and "major bottleneck," pointing out that a large bottleneck would allow traffic to flow smoothly.

Soft Shoulders

Brawny and hard-working, yet compassionate, our shoulders bear arms, responsibilities and sometimes the weight of the world with admirable resilience. Shoulders are where we show confidence, comfort loved ones and display patches of loyalty. Given these diverse associations, it's no wonder the word *shoulder* (from the Old English *sculdor*) has produced so many idiomatic expressions.

cold shoulder—During medieval times, it was customary for traveling knights to be offered a hot meal at any home they visited. Householders would keep generous cuts of warm mutton and beef on the fire in hopes of feeding a knight. But gradually this hospitable tradition died, and soon journeying jousters were being treated, not to warm cuts of prime rib, but to last week's leftovers, including cold shoulders and shanks. By the early 1800s, "give the cold shoulder" had come to mean ignore or exclude someone we don't like.

a chip on the shoulder—There are at least two red-blooded, full-bearded derivations of this American expression for what we would call today "copping an attitude." According to the rules of a nineteenth-century American game (known for its sophistication and subtlety), one person would place a block of wood on his shoulder and dare someone to knock it off. The person who knocked the other guy's block the farthest distance won. Thus anyone who was spoiling for a fight was said to have a "chip on his shoulder." But others say this idiom evolved among lumberjacks who became annoyed when careless colleagues, cutting in trees above them, dropped wood chips onto their shoulders.

straight from the shoulder—This idiom comes from the boxing ring, where a fighter sometimes delivers a punch directly from the shoulder without swinging his arm away from the body. There's nothing subtle about such a blow, so "straight from the shoulder" has come to mean any statement or action that's powerful and direct.

Face-Off

A newspaper once reported that a campus look-alike contest was adjudicated by two cross-dressing male judges who were the "spit and image" of Leona Helmsley. (Considering Helmsley's reputation as the "Queen of Mean," these cross-dressers were probably very cross, indeed.)

Our subject here, however, is not our Leona's venomous spite, but our language's venerable *spit and image*. Should this phrase, meaning exact likeness, be *spit and image* or *spitting image*? And how did it dribble into our language?

Because *spit and image* is the spit and image of *spitting image*, either term is acceptable in spoken or written English.

Spitting image, used much more commonly now, is actually a corruption of the older phrase *spit and image*, which first appeared in England during the early nineteenth century. While purists of yore favored *spit and image* over *spitting image*, today's experts prefer the latter.

Seeking this phrase's origins, scholars have assembled a virtual salivation army of possible explanations:

> ➤ Etymologist Charles Funk noted that *spit* has long meant an exact replica in English. In the early nineteenth-century England, for instance, people would describe a look-alike son as "the spit of his father." (Knowing, as we do now, that saliva contains a person's DNA, this might actually be true.) Funk suggested Americans probably added the redundant "and image" to *spit* to reinforce the precise resemblance.

> ➤ Newspaper columnist O. O. McIntyre speculated that *spit and image* may have been an African-American rendering of *spirit and image*, a term indicating the child possessed both the spirit as well as the appearance of the parent.

> ➤ Writer John Ciardi attributed the phrase to black magic. The material used to make hex dolls, he noted, often included hair, fingernail parings and spit from the intended victim. Thus, such a doll was literally the victim's spit and image.

Another face-saving term is *deadpan*. A kitchen pan, with its round shape and skinny handle, resembles a human head and neck, so it's not surprising *pan* came to mean face. In 1864, for instance, Abraham Lincoln, well known for his skill-et concealment, said he was resolved to be very "shut pan" about a matter, meaning he'd maintain a poker face. (By the way, *pan* isn't the only association of kitchen items with the face; a person with an attractive *mug* is a *dish* with whom we want to *spoon*.)

It wasn't until the 1920s, however, that English first saw *deadpan* walking. The term was first associated only with acting, but then became pandemic. In 1929, the newspaper *Variety* referred to the "dead-pan comic's expression." The greatest deadpan-handler of all, of course, was the miserly Jack Benny.

Humor Me

During the Middle Ages, doctors and philosophers believed people's moods were controlled by four main liquids, or humors, in the body: phlegm, blood, black bile and yellow bile. When a person's behavior indicated an excess of one of these humors, medieval physicians worked them over like the mechanics in one of those fifteen-minute oil and lube shops. They would drain a patient's blood, administer laxatives and give emetics until they felt they had achieved the proper balance of humors. If a person's humors were in balance, he was said to be in "good humor."

phlegmatic—People who were sleepy, sluggish and unemotional were thought to have a surplus of phlegm, so today the adjective *phlegmatic* means impassive, stolid, apathetic.

sanguine—Happy, exuberant people were believed to have an excess of blood, giving them reddish faces. These Pollyannas were said to be *sanguine* (from *sanquis*, Latin for blood), and we still use this word to describe someone with a cheerful temperament or a ruddy complexion.

bilious—Cranky, cross people were believed to be suffering from an excess of bile, and *bilious* still means ill tempered or peevish.

melancholic—Another symptom of too much black bile was depression, so people who were gloomy were said to be suffering from *melancholy*, from the Greek *melan* (dark) and *chole* (bile).

choleric—Too much yellow bile was thought to make a person angry and we still describe a hot-tempered person as *choleric*.

Brain Drain

Sometimes being smart can smart. Just think of the epithets intelligent people endure. We all admire—and hate—the smartest kid in the class, and one heady way to express this ambivalence is to associate a high IQ with a misshapen skull.

Thus, we call smart people *long heads* (because they take the long view), *pointy heads* (as if heads could be sharpened like pencils), *highbrows* (large forehead equals large intelligence), and *egg heads* (oval-shaped crania hatch brainy ideas).

The most famous American egghead, Democratic presidential candidate Adlai Stevenson, once cracked, "Eggheads unite! You have nothing to lose but your yokes." Unfortunately, this "yoke" laid an egg with American voters who weren't about to put someone as smart as he was in charge of the country. Enter Ike.

As for gray matters, *brain* might seem like a fine term for a smart person, but using a part to describe a whole (a literary technique called *synecdoche*) can really brain a person. I mean, imagine calling a soccer player a "foot," a violinist an "arm" or a baby a "stomach"? Likewise, *intellectual* and *intelligentsia* pack elitist connotations, and, in psychology, *intellectualization* is an undesirable defense against real feelings. More recently, *wonk* has succeeded *dweeb*, *grind* and *nerd* as the insult-of-choice to describe the studious.

Even our positive metaphors for intelligence have become clichés. The two most common phrases for a no-brainer project are the shopworn "This isn't brain surgery" and "It doesn't take a rocket scientist." Given the smart bombs dropping around us, it doesn't take a rocket scientist to see that we need some new terms for bright people. But, then again, I'm no brain surgeon.

Body Piercing

Pierce the surface of these words and you'll discover a body part.

When supercilious snobs disapprove of something—say, body piercing—they often raise their eyebrows in haughty disdain. In fact, *supercilious* comes from the Latin word for eyebrow—*supercilium*, a combo of *super-* (above) and *cilium* (eyelid).

A gorgeous woman might have a beautiful throat, among other things. That's appropriate, for *gorgeous* derives from the Late Latin *gurges*, throat. In Middle French, *gorgias* referred to a garment that covered the throat and shoulders. Soon an especially decorative *gorgias* became a sign of wealth, and *gorgias* came to mean elegant, fashionable, and, eventually, beautiful.

Sarcasm can cut you to the quick. So you won't be surprised to learn that the word *sarcasm* derives from the Greek *sarx*, meaning flesh. *Sarx* produced the Greek verb *sarkazein*, meaning "to tear flesh like dogs," and from *sarkazein* came the Greek noun *sarkasmos*, meaning the same thing as its English descendent, *sarcasm*.

Another English word derived from the Greek *sarx* is *sarcophagus*. The ancient Greeks used a certain kind of limestone to make coffins because they believed it hastened the decomposition of the body. This stone was called *sarcophagus lapis*, literally, "flesh-eating stone." So in Latin and later in English, *sarcophagus* came to mean any stone coffin, even if it didn't devour the dead.

If you're about to be inoculated by a doctor, you're likely to fix your eye on that big needle coming toward you. That's understandable, for *inoculate* derives from *oculus*, the Latin word for eye. The Romans also used *oculus* to mean bud, because they thought the buds of plants resembled human eyes. In fact, the process of grafting an *oculus* from one plant to another became known as *inoculatio*.

During the 1700s, when doctors began injecting people with small amounts of a germ to protect them from getting the full-blown disease caused by the germ, they saw parallels to the horticultural process of grafting. So they called the procedure *inoculation*—yet another form of body piercing.

Left-Handed Compliments

And now a heated debate between Lefty Lingo and Righty Rhetoric . . .

Lefty: When it comes to creating words, lefties rule! The Latin word *sinister*, for instance, originally meant left or on the left side. But, because most righties were inept at using their left hands, *sinister* came to mean awkward, and eventually injurious, evil.

Righty: That Latin leftover is nothing compared to *dexterous*. In Latin, *dexter* meant related to or located on the right, and, because most people are more proficient with their right hands, *dexterous* came to mean skillful, deft. And someone who uses both hands as if they were right hands is *ambidextrous*, from *ambi* (both) and *dexter* (right).

Lefty: Right. But we lefties coined the word *awkward* for someone with two left feet. In Middle English *awke* meant from the left or backhanded, and *awkward* meant in an awke direction. So any backhanded sword stroke, for instance, was called an "awkward stroke," whether it was skillful or clumsy. But eventually *awkward* came to mean ungraceful or uncomfortable.

Righty: You've exhausted your *left* bank, but I turn to the Left Bank where the French word *droit* shares many meanings with the English *right*. The French phrase *a droit* means properly, and in English *adroit* means skillful.

Lefty: But in French the left-handed "complement" of *adroit* is *gauche*, meaning left. In English, the meaning of *gauche* has expanded to include tactless, crude, tasteless.

Righty: Enough of your leftism! Did you know that scientists named a form of glucose *dextrose* because its plane of polarization is rotated toward the right? Biologically this is important because the body processes dextrose differently from similar forms of sugar that rotate the plane of polarization to the left.

Lefty: Speaking of rotation, a left-hander in a baseball team's pitching rotation is called a *southpaw*. The standard explanation for this term is that many baseball diamonds are laid out so batters face east and don't have to squint into the afternoon sun. Thus, the pitcher faces west with the left arm on the south side.

But hard proof of this theory has gone south, and the explanation that's right may have . . . er . . . left.

Heart-to-Heart Talk

When you speak before a large audience (gulp!), your heart is often in your mouth—in more ways than you might think. The Latin and Greek roots for *heart* throb in scores of English words.

Many of these words wear their hearts on their sleeves. Someone with courage, for instance, has a stout heart. So it's not surprising that the word *courage* derives, through the Middle English *corage*, from the Latin root for heart, *cor*.

Likewise, a cordial person is warm-hearted. The agreeable words *accord* and *concord* refer to being of one heart, while *discord* denotes hostile hearts.

Heart-related medical terms such as *cardiac, cardiogram* and *pericardium* come straight from the Greek heart—*kardia*. But it takes a cardiogram to find the heart in *quarry*, meaning a hunted animal or prey. *Quarry* evolved from *cor*, via a series of intestine-like twists and turns through the Vulgar Latin *corata* (viscera) to the Middle English *querre* (entrails).

(But, no, the *quarry* that means rock pit has nothing to do with having a heart of stone. That *quarry* is extracted from the Latin *quadrum*, square, because stone is often cut into square pieces.)

Credit, credo and *credible* come from the Latin *credere* (to entrust), believed to be a combination of the Indo-European roots *kerd-* (heart) and *dhe* (to place). So when you extend *credit* to someone, you place your heart (and money) in his hands. Gulp!

Our phrase "learn it by heart" provides a clue to the cardio-vascular origins of *record*. It's derived from the Latin *recordari*, a combination of *re-* (again) and *cor* (heart). So something that's recorded is "in the heart again."

But when you examine *coronary*, bypass the notion it's derived from *cor*. Because the arteries and veins of the heart resemble crowns, these structures were named for the Latin word for crown, *corona*.

And, no, coroners are not so called because they examine the bodies of those whose hearts have stopped. *Coroner* comes from the Latin *custos placitorum coronae* (guardian of the crown's pleas). The original coroners performed a variety of legal functions, including investigations of suspicious deaths. Later, this became their main, well, beat—or lack thereof.

A Riff on Midriff

As if you hadn't noticed, American girls and women are baring their equatorial latitude with attitude. Of course, we dispassionate scholars in the word-watching trade ogle . . . er . . . observe these peekaboo tummies with purely academic interest. So, before this trend goes belly-up, let's bare the origins of the word *midriff*.

Four hundred years ago, viewing an exposed *midriff* would have induced not lust, but disgust. That's because, from the 1100s until the 1930s, *midriff* denoted the diaphragm, the muscle that expands and contracts the lungs. (Because the diaphragm forms a wall between the thoracic and abdominal cavities, *midriff*, for a few centuries at least, was also a general term for a partition or barrier.)

It wasn't until the 1930s that *midriff* was turned inside out. Influenced by the more revealing fashions of the twentieth century, *midriff* came to refer to the outside of the torso's midsection, or to clothing covering (or exposing) it, as in, "She's wearing a diaphanous midriff." But the new meaning of *midriff* and its old meaning of the diaphragm do have one thing in common: they both induce heavy breathing.

Similarly, several other words for body parts have shimmied and shifted in meaning over the years. Until *belly* went on a diet during the 1500s, for instance, it referred to the entire body, not just the abdomen. This meaning survives in the agricultural term *pork belly*, meaning not just to the abdomen of a butchered pig but the entire side of the animal. Likewise, *knuckle* once denoted not just the finger joint, but any joint in the body, including the elbow or knee. That's why *knuckle under* (to bend one's knees) means to submit or give in to someone.

Before the 1300s, anyone who spoke the word *gum* was saying a mouthful. That's because *gum* originally referred not only to the flesh in which the teeth are fixed, but also to the inside of the entire mouth and throat. Similarly, until the 1600s, *nerve* meant not the body's delicate filaments of sensation, but its brawny sinews and tendons, and we still use the phrase "strain every nerve" to describe extreme muscular exertion.

Did you know lungs were once called *lights* because of their light weight? This old meaning of *lights* still survives in the threat. "Stare at my midriff once more, and I'll punch your lights out."

Bon Mot Voyage!
Words of Boats, Trains, Cars, and Planes

When it comes to words derived from transportation, English is a moveable feast. You probably won't be *taken aback* to find that nautical terms have been a *mainstay* of English, that railroad express-ions have taken the *fast track* to popularity, or that much airplane terminal-ology has *taken off*. No wonder so many English words simply "trip" off our tongues.

Shipshape

Because Great Britain and the United States have always been sea-faring nations, it's not surprising that many terms for sailing tactics have navigated their way into English. The nautical origins of colloquial mainstays like *take a different tack* and *learn the ropes* are readily apparent, but you may be taken aback by the salty sources of others.

mainstay—Since the mainstay is the strong rope that helps to support a ship's main mast, *mainstay* has come to mean anything that provides primary support.

cut and run—This term, describing someone's hasty and often cowardly exit from a perilous situation, is anchored in the quick getaways made by ships at anchorage. Instead of wasting time weighing anchor ("Yup, still fifteen hundred pounds, Captain!"), sailors in a hurry simply cut the anchor cable and sail speedily away. (I wonder if sailors on a warship that had cut and run replaced their anchor with a proverbial *loose cannon*.)

taken aback—If a ship is not handled properly during tacking (shifting its course), the wind may strike the front of its sails, pushing it backward. This is not a good thing; the mast could break. A ship in this plight is said to be *taken aback*, as is anyone who is thrown off balance by a sudden remark or event.

squared away—When the wind is directly behind a square-rigged ship, its yards (spars holding the sails) are set at right angles to the ship's centerline. The yards are then said to be *squared away*, now a general term for anything put in proper order.

back and fill—In narrow channels or rivers, square riggers moving against the wind have to maneuver by *backing* (literally sailing stern first), hauling the yards around, and then *filling* (sailing bow first). Given the laborious, back-and-forth motion of such a course, it's not surprising that *back and fill* now means to vacillate or act indecisively.

aloof—If a ship is being driven into shore by a strong wind, there is no choice but to *luff*, to steer as closely into the wind as possible. If the helmsperson falls off this optimum course, the captain may frantically call out "Aluff!" which means "steer closer to the wind." Thus, *aloof* came to describe a person who, like a ship staying away from a rocky shore, keeps an emotional distance from others.

tide over—Because sandbars block the entrances to many harbors and rivers, ships cannot enter them until these barriers *tide over* (are covered to a sufficient depth by the incoming tide.) So anything that *tides us over* (like a loan from Dad), helps get us through a difficulty, from bar bills to bar exams.

in the offing—Sailors refer to the part of the sea that's off in the distance but still visible near the horizon as the *offing*. Because an approaching ship first appears in the offing, we now describe any upcoming event as being *in the offing*.

by and large—When a square-rigged sailing ship tacks into the wind, the skipper will order a seasoned helmsperson to steer *full and by*, that is, by the wind (as close to the wind's direction as possible) while still keeping the sails full. But an inexperienced helmsperson, who might have trouble with this difficult maneuver, will be ordered to steer *by and large*, that is, by the wind but not too close to it. Thus *by and large* has come to mean loosely or generally speaking.

touch and go—When a ship scrapes its keel on a reef or sand-bar but sails on without much damage or loss of velocity, it is said to *touch and go*. We now use this term to describe any precarious situation or narrow escape.

In fact, things are still touch and go for this derivation. Some experts say the term comes from stagecoach days when drivers often bumped wheels while passing each other on narrow roads. (Think of the wheel-to-wheel chariot race in the movie *Ben-Hur;* now *that* was a touch-and-go situation.

take someone down a peg—The colors (flags and pennants) flown on a ship are raised and lowered by pegs. So when a high-flying flag is lowered to a position of less prominence, it's said to be *taken down a peg*, a term that has come to mean to deflate or humble someone.

bitter end—On a ship, the *bitts* are the strong posts on the deck to which chains or cables are attached. When the anchor chain has been stretched to the limit, its *bitts end* or *bitter end* has been exposed, giving us the term's present meaning of the final stages or any protracted struggle.

get down to brass tacks—Etymologists surmise that the *brass tacks* referred to in this expression are the copper bolts on the hull of a ship, which are exposed when the hull is completely scraped of barnacles. Thus, someone who clears away all debris and gets to the bottom of something is *getting down to brass tacks*.

posh—The story usually given for the origin of this term is literally too good to be true. The tale goes that wealthy English travelers booking sea passage to India would always try to reserve staterooms on the shady, and therefore, more comfortable side of the ship. Thus they requested "Port Out, Starboard Home," meaning they wanted to be on the port side on the eastbound, outward journey and the starboard side on the

15

westbound, homebound voyage. Tickets for these more expensive rooms were thus stamped with the acronym "P.O.S.H." and *posh* became a synonym for elegant and fashionable.

Unfortunately, linguists can find no evidence to support the P.O.S.H. derivation for *posh*. They offer much more boring, landlubber explanations that *posh* was British slang for money or that it once meant *dandy*.

devil to pay—Many popular books on word origins will tell you that the expressions *the devil to pay* and *between the devil and the deep blue sea* derive, not from the naughty devil, but from the nautical *devil*. Sure enough, the *devil* is a sailor's term for a seam in a ship's hull. And *pay* does mean to apply pitch. So some say *pay the devil* originally referred to spreading pitch on a hull's seam to keep it watertight. Likewise, *between the devil and the deep blue sea* is said to refer to the space between such a seam and the ocean, a precarious place indeed.

It's a hull of a theory, but it's almost certainly wrong. The first recorded use of *devil* to mean the seam on a hull didn't occur until 1828. Yet the expressions *the devil to pay* and *between the devil and the deep blue sea* were first recorded in the 1500s and 1600s, respectively. It's possible, of course, that sailors used *devil* to mean a hull's seam for many years, perhaps several decades, before this term was written down. But a gap of three centuries between oral use and written use is hard to explain. More likely, the *devil* in these expressions is the Old Deceiver himself.

Skull and Crosswords

Arrrgghh, mateys! It's time we heaved to for some pirate talk!

Buccaneers rarely barbecued their victims (and when they did, they barbecued them rare). But the word *buccaneer* originally meant barbecuer. During the 1600s, French and English renegades, who lived as woodsmen and herdsmen on the Caribbean island of Hispañola, used a rack called a *boucan* to smoke meat, and thus called themselves *boucaners*. When a Spanish treasure ship sailed by, these *boucaners* would attack it, becoming the swashbuckling *buccaneers* we know and love.

(Leaving no swash unbuckled, I'll note that the noun *swash* was coined to imitate the sound of a hit or blow. A *buckler* was a small, round shield carried or worn on the arm. So a *swashbuckler* was someone whose sword made great swashes as it struck the opponent's buckler. By extension, *swashbuckler* came to mean any swaggering show-off.)

Another name for pirate, *freebooter*, conjures up images of a buccaneer's big black boots. In fact, the *boot* in *freebooter* (from the Dutch *vrijbuit*) refers, not to the pirate's boot but to his loot. A *freebooter* freely takes booty. That booty often included *pieces of eight*, silver Spanish coins so named because they were worth eight Spanish reales. Often these pieces of eight were themselves cut up into pieces, creating a piece of a piece of eight.

Now for a skull session: While pirates did fly the skull and crossbones and engage in skullduggery, there's no connection between the two terms. *Skullduggery*, meaning *crafty deception, trickery*, is an alteration of the Scots word *sculdudrie*, meaning . . . well, guess how little pirates are made.

Speaking of which, some licentious linguists speculate that *Jolly Roger*, the term for a pirate flag, was a euphemism for a certain male organ. Others call this theory phall-acious, noting that *Roger* was simply a generic term for any male, as *Jack* or *Mac* is today. Whether the original Roger was a pirate crew member—or the member of a pirate crew member—the true etymology of *Jolly Roger* has apparently walked the plank.

Steamboat Gossip

As stern-wheelers and side-wheelers churned our waterways during the nineteenth century, they churned up new terms as well, permanently wrinkling the ol' man river of American English. Every time we complain that an athlete is *showboating*, talk of *hitting a snag*, or call our ne'er-do-well brother-in-law a *roustabout*, we've committed a mighty Mississ-slip of the tongue.

Vigilant steamboat captains continuously scanned the river for *snags*—uprooted trees that had become stuck in the riverbed. And we still say that a project encountering difficulties has *hit a snag*. (And when this happens, we say a lot of other words once uttered by steamboat deckhands.)

Steamboat pilots became such connoisseurs of snags, in fact, that they coined special terms to denote the peculiarities of these obstacles. Pieces of timber that bobbed up and down in the river, as if praying, were called *passengers* . . . er . . . *preachers*. Similarly, trunks and branches that looked like saws cutting across the rippling current were called *sawyers*. (This term may have inspired the name of Mark Twain's character Tom Sawyer who, come to think of it, is a little wooden.)

As every school child learns, Samuel Clemens lifted his pen name *Mark Twain* from steamboat terminology as well. Steamboats often navigated in shallow water, where running aground was a danger. So a crewmember called a *leadsman* regularly measured the water's depth with a pole or a weighted line, and then shouted the depth to the pilot. When the depth was one fathom (six feet), the leadsman would call out, "mark one," for two fathoms, "mark twain," and so on. The deepest sounding was "mark four," and, after that the cry was "no bottom," which, thankfully, Clemens didn't choose as a pseudonym.

The steamboat's voracious boilers gulped enormous quantities of wood, so captains stopped frequently at wood yards along the riverbank to *wood up*. During such pit stops, passengers would disembark to stroll along the riverbank and enjoy libations—so many libations, in fact, that *to wood up* became a common American expression for to get drunk.

Steamboat deckhands were such a motley assortment of vagabonds, drifters and renegades that they soon earned their own term: *roustabouts*. (Probably, many of these unsavory deckhands had already earned—and served—several terms.) *Roustabout*, which was derived from the old verb *rouse* (to arouse, stir up) and its variant *roust*, would eventually come to describe a wide variety of roving, unskilled laborers, including longshoremen, oil field workers, circus hands and dot.com executives.

A new term was also invented to describe passengers who could afford only standing room on the steamboat—*standees*. By contrast, wealthy passengers stayed in staterooms that were, literally, state rooms—they were named for the states of the Union. The captain's cabin, usually the largest stateroom, was named for a large state—Texas—and the porch next to the captain's quarters was *the Texas deck* (now a favorite barbecue spot at the western White House). The highest and longest deck, where the wealthiest passengers promenaded, was called the *hurricane deck*, possibly because of the strong breeze created by the fast-moving boat (or was it hot air generated by the pompous promenaders themselves?).

Some steamboats, with their wedding-cake decorations and gingerbread details, became so elaborate and fashionable that architects began imitating this look on Victorian houses across the United States. This domestic style became known as *steamboat Gothic*, which, come to think of it, would be a great name for a punk rock band.

The most flamboyant type of steamboat was the showboat. These floating theaters, which began plying the Mississippi after the Civil War, staged everything from Shakesperean tragedies to melodramas to vaudeville acts (but, surprisingly, no *Riverdance*). To attract audiences, these productions became more and more elaborate and elegant, as did the showboats themselves, some seating up to three hundred people, not to mention the river pirates.

So it's no surprise that the verb *showboat* evolved, meaning to act in a conspicuous or ostentatious way, to hotdog. What's not clear is whether this verb, or its noun form *showboater*, is based on the embellishments of the showboats themselves or of the shows they presented. For now, we'll give these two explanations double-billing.

Locomotive Locutions

Many railroad terms have *made the grade* in common American English. Phrases like *sidetrack*, *derail*, *streamline* and *end of the line* chug through our language. Among today's *fast track* business people, for instance, the hip term for a huge disaster is *train wreck*. Here are some other choo-choo-isms to chew on:

hell on wheels—When railroads were being built across the American West, gangs of construction workers often lived in boxcars along the route. Joined by wagonloads of gamblers, liquor sellers, prostitutes and other hangers-on, they formed a rolling, rollicking town that moved continually down the line as construction progressed. Because of its riotous revelry, such a portable community was called a *hell on wheels*, a phrase we still apply to any person, place or event noted for boisterous or reckless behavior.

gravy train—In common American speech, *gravy* has long meant easy money. Thus, railroad workers referred to a short haul that paid well as a *gravy run* or *gravy train*, a term that still refers to any source of high income for little effort.

jerkwater town—Early steam engines needed enormous amounts of water. If a small town along a railroad was not big enough to be a *tank town* (a town with a water tower for steam engines), a long metal trough filled with water was placed between the rails. As a train passed, a scoop lowered beneath the locomotive jerked water from the trough. Because trains stopped in tank towns but not in jerkwater towns, the former enjoyed a somewhat higher, if less splashy, reputation.

highball—A large ball hoisted to the top of a station's signal mast told engineers that they could proceed without stopping. Thus, to *highball* came to mean to speed. Any connection between the railroad term and the tall whiskey cocktail called a *highball* is uncertain, but some speculate that the ice cube floating at the top of the glass resembled a railroad highball at the top of its mast.

Calling All Cars

Did you know the name *Corvair* was a blend of two other Chevrolet models (Corvette and Bel Air)? That the Plymouth was named for the rock-like endurance of the Pilgrims?

And that creators of the Ford Fiesta fawned over the name *Bambi* until Henry Ford II shot it down? Here's a bumper crop of car names:

Just about everyone knows the Ford Motor Company committed vehicular "nomicide" by nepotistically naming the Edsel after Henry Ford's son. But did you know Ford executives Lew Veraldi and John Risk called their new model the *Taurus* because both their wives were born under the zodiac sign of Taurus? That's no bull.

Of equally stellar origin is *Subaru*, which means the Pleiades in Japanese, the constellation of stars appearing on the car's logo. Speaking of Japanese, *Mitsubishi* means three pebbles (portrayed as three diamonds on its logo). And, if the name *Isuzu* rings a bell, it may be because *Isuzu* means fifty bells.

One of the great folk legends regarding a Japanese *nom de fume* goes like this: Nissan executives once called a German consultant and told him they needed a name for a new car fast—in one day. "Ach, mein goodness," replied the German, "Dat sun!" (In fact, *Datsun* is based on *DAT*, from the initials of the firm's three founding investors.)

Chicago Tribune writer Dan Tucker points out the illogic of the car name *Reliant*, which, when you think about it, means dependent on someone else.

Other motory monikers:

➤ Ford was gun shy of *Colt* because the name was associated with revolvers, but that didn't stop Chrysler from using it.

➤ Studebaker's *Dictator* model rose to power in the 1930s until the company deposed it with a "coupe" in 1938.

➤ Chrysler's K-car of the 1980s took its name from the code letter of its test prototype, but, considering Chrysler's federal bailout at the time, some suggested it be called the "IOU car."

Plane English

Let's consider some high-flying terms.

To pilots, passengers are *dogs*, *geese* and *paxes* (from *PAX*, the ticket code for passengers). Frequent fliers are *crash bait*, and a passenger who causes trouble is a *hawk* or *vulture*. Tourist class is *the back of the bus*, *cattle class* or *the wrong side of the curtain*.

The controlled airspace around an airport is the *birdcage*; a flight on which many passengers become airsick is a *blow show*; a near collision with another airplane is *counting the rivets* (as in, so close you can count the rivets of the other plane); the choice between filet mignon and chicken cordon bleu offered to pilots is *leather or feather*; and an inactive runway where an incoming plane waits for an available gate is the *penalty box*.

Among military pilots, taking a nap is *checking for light leaks;* jet fuel is *go juice*; and an aircraft that needs continual repairs is a *hangar queen*. A thousand feet of altitude is an *angel*, so *angels fifteen* means 15,000 feet above sea level; a hundred feet of altitude is a *cherub*, so *four cherubs* means four hundred feet. And any pilot who ejects from the cockpit becomes a lifetime member of the *Martin-Baker Fan Club*, named for the company that manufactures ejection seats.

Other plane-spoken terms include:

the Clampetts—Families who've never flown before (from the last name of TV's "Beverly Hillbillies")

ramp rats, also ***rampies***—baggage handlers, especially non-union contract laborers brought in to handle cargo

the blue room—airplane lavatory, named for the blue disinfectant used in its toilet

bump and jump—a touch and go landing

airside—the runway area of the tarmac, as opposed to the taxiways

plane mate—waiting room on wheels mounted on a jack-knife-like structure

let's kick the tire and light the fire—pilot's slang for "Let's start the engines and take off." Similar phrases include "It's wheels in the well time" (departure time) and "Put the rubber side down" (lower the landing gear).

rotation—the moment during take-off when the lift from the wings takes effect and the plane's weight rotates from the nose gear to the main landing gear.

roach coach—catering truck that delivers meals to planes.

baloney—tanker truck carrying aviation fuel (after its tubular shape). Though composed mostly of kerosene, aviation fuel is called *oil*.

yield control—attempts by airlines to manage no-shows for reservations and keep planes full without bumping anyone.

pushing tin—what air traffic controllers call their job.

speed bird—nickname for the Concorde and all British Airways planes (from the swooping logo on the old British Overseas Airways planes).

By the way, the British objected so strongly to the Frenchified "e" at the end of *Concorde* that they almost pulled out of their deal with France to build and operate the plane. Trying to save face, Prime Minister Harold MacMillan patriotically proclaimed, "The 'e' shall stand for 'England'!"

And two aviation terms have recently flown into general parlance:

cutting edge—This expression most likely descends from *leading edge*, a term that originally referred to the blade of ship's propeller, then to the wings of airplanes and later to the electronic blips sent out by radar. During the 1950s, people started using *cutting edge* to describe something in the forefront of technology.

pushing the envelope—The term may have originated in mathematics where *envelope* refers to the boundary of a group of equations or curves. Those who link it to ballooning, where the craft's gas or air container is called an *envelope*, may be full of hot air. But there's no doubt it jetted into popular parlance from aeronautics where *pushing the envelope* means to fly a plane to the limits of its capabilities.

HOUSEHOLD WORDS

Words to Live By

Did you know the word *economy* comes from the Greek word for management of a family? The Greek *oikonomous*, a combination of oikos (house) and *nemein* (to manage) means one who manages. *Oikos* is housed in several other English words bearing the sense of habitation or lair (*diocese, ecology, ecumenical*), while *nemein*, meaning distribute or allocate, survives in *Nemesis*, the Greek goddess who distributed bad fortune to the boastful and proud. Let's look at some other words related to the household.

Verbal Room-inations

Did you know that there's a fire in your *foyer* and wind in your *window*? And, no, I'm not selling smoke alarms or insulation. *Foyer*, for instance, comes from the Old French *foier* (fireplace) and the Latin *focus* (hearth). Thus, this entrance room, which sometimes has a fireplace, is a focal point where people gather.

Window descends from the Old Norse *vindagauga*, which meant wind's eye. Before the invention of glass, windows were indeed places where you could get an eyeful of wind, especially if they were located in a high structure (see *Eyeful Tower*).

Like most words used in everyday life, our words for the rooms and parts of a house are among the oldest in English. *House* itself comes directly from the Old English *hus*, which is also the root word of *husband* (house owner). Likewise, *roof, room* and *hearth* are remodeled versions of the Old English words *hrof, rum* and *heorth*, respectively, while *cellar, vestibule* and *kitchen* descend from Latin: *cella* (storage room), *vestibulum*

25

(entrance hall) and *coquinus* (cooking). *Pantry,* a storage area for food, is based on the Latin *pan* (bread).

A *drawing room* has nothing to do with drawing, but a lot to do with withdrawing. It's a shortening of *withdrawing room,* a room to which guests withdraw for formal receptions. A similar room is a *parlor,* where people parley (talk), from the French *parler,* to speak. In medieval times, a *parlatorium* was a special room in a monastery where monks could temporarily suspend their vows of silence by speaking with outsiders.

There's even a story in *story* (the level of a house). *Story* comes from the Latin *historia,* the same word that gives us *history* and *story.* In antiquity, painted windows and sculptures on each floor of a building often told a story, so each level became known as a *story.*

Finally, lets go "up attic," as New Englanders say, to find another art-related term. The ancient Athenians developed a distinct style of architecture called *Attic,* named for the peninsula where they lived. Because the decorative structures sitting at the top of classical buildings were often designed in the Attic style, the upper portion of any building soon came to be called the *attic.* Personally, I've always liked the Attic style. Call me a "fan-Attic" or simply an "Attic fan."

Couch It in These Terms

No furniture store offers better word origins than The Word Guy's Discount Furniture Barn. With each piece you buy, you get a free explanation of its name!

Check out this cute little *credenza.* In medieval times, kings and queens were constantly worried about being poisoned. So, before they dined, their food was placed on a small sideboard where the royal taster tasted it. Because this piece of furniture served as a test site for the food's trustworthiness, it became known as a *credentia,* Medieval Latin for trust.

How about a *chesterfield*? This sofa is named for the nineteenth-century earl of Chesterfield. Like the earl himself, it's slightly overstuffed. Probably because of its English origins, *chesterfield* is a generic term for couch in Canada. Sofa, so good.

But why Californians' discussions of couches are couched in terms like *chesterfield* isn't known "fer shure."

To go with your new *davenport* (a type of sofa probably named for its manufacturer), how about a *hassock*? Hassocks are so called because they resemble the dense clumps of grass known as hassocks, from *hassuc*, an Old English word for sedge, a type of grasslike plant. And if you don't know that *ottoman*, the name for another type of footstool, comes from Turkey's Ottoman Empire, you ought to, man.

Or perhaps you'd prefer a canopy bed. The etymology of *canopy* involves entomology. Ancient Greek armies were constantly annoyed by mosquitoes, which may explain why they had so many swat teams. Soon soldiers began placing netting over their beds to keep the pests out. They called these coverings *konopeion*, after *konops*, the Greek word for mosquito, and *konopeion* still buzzes over our heads in *canopy*, which came to denote an ornamental, rooflike structure or a cloth covering over a bed.

How about a nice bureau? The word *bureau* has grown, well, like a bureaucracy. In medieval France, a *burel* was simply a coarse cloth covering for a desk. But soon, in a departmental reorganization, *burel* became *bureau*, and *bureau* came to refer, not only to the cloth covering the desk, but also to the desk itself and eventually to the whole office.

Words Out of Sink

"Why do you call yourself a plumber?" I once asked my plumber. At the time, he was performing an esoteric procedure under my sink involving a hose, a drill and an amorphous mass of glop. "Hey, buddy, I ain't *that* bad," he replied defensively, not realizing I was asking about the origin of the word *plumber*.

So I had to look it up myself. *Plumber* comes from the Latin *plumbum*, meaning the metal lead. In Roman times most pipes and fixtures for carrying water in a building were made of lead. So a person who worked on these fittings was a *plumbarius*, which became *plumber* in English and "This is gonna cost ya" in American.

A plumber who wants to determine exact vertical direction drops a *plumb line*. It's so called because the first plumb lines consisted of a string attached to a lead weight. This sense of exactness survives in the adverb *plumb*, meaning precisely, completely. Which explains why we say to our plumber, "If you think I'm going to pay this bill, you're plumb crazy."

Toilet comes from the Roman *tela* (cloth) which became *toile* in Middle French. The diminutive *toilette* meant a little cloth for covering a dressing table, and eventually came to refer to the dressing table itself. The English adopted *toilette* as *toilet*. But soon King John and the magistrates of his notorious "star-chamber" pot changed the meaning of *toilet* from dressing table, to dressing room with bath facilities, to bathroom, and finally to the john itself. And if this sequence of meanings seems to keep running, just jiggle the handle.

True or false?: The origin of *faucet* is *false*.

True! It's *false*. The Latin verb *falsare* (to falsify) became *fausser* in French. Eventually *fausser* came to mean to damage or break. Because a stopper plugging a cask containing liquid seemed to pierce or break into the cask, that stopper became known as a *fausset*. Soon *fausset* leaked into English where it came to mean not only the stopper in a cask, but a device for draining water from the cask. And that's the origin of everything but the kitchen sink.

Term Mights

Ah, home ownership—the great American dream of escaping your landlord, carrying your spouse over the threshold, and signing a thirty-year mortgage! But when you find out where the words *landlord*, *threshold* and *mortgage* come from, you may want to go back to paying rent.

There's probably no more terrifying word in English than *landlord*, but the *lord* part of this word, at least, once denoted a benign provider. *Lord* is a compression of the Old English *hlaford*, which, in turn, comes from two Old English words: *hlaf*, meaning loaf of bread, and *weard*, meaning keeper or guard. So a lord was literally the bread keeper, and, by extension, a head of household. (In fact, to this day, some landlords are loafers.)

Threshold, meaning the sill of a door, is indeed related to *thresh*, meaning to beat stems and husks to separate grain from straw. In olden days, this threshing was often performed by the feet of oxen or of people. And so *thresh* came to be associated with part of the door continually being trampled. (Etymologists are still threshing out the origin of the *hold* part of *threshold*, while entomologists are still threshing out the origins of termites in thresholds.)

Did someone say "*termites*"?!

And if your mortgage payment mortifies you, that's linguistically appropriate. For the *mort* in *mortgage* indeed refers to death. *Mortgage* is a combination of *mort*, meaning dead, and *gage*, meaning pledge. The concept of death comes into the word *mortgage* in two ways: 1) If the buyer doesn't make the mortgage payments, the mortgagee reclaims the land; so the land is "dead" to the buyer. 2) And if the buyer does make all the payments, the agreement becomes "dead" to the mortgagee, and a nice little source of monthly income ceases. And, in case you're wondering, *mortgagor* refers to the person who mortgages his property (the borrower), while *mortgagee* refers to the person to whom property is mortgaged (the lender).

An even more mortifying real estate term is *mortmain*, which refers to the perpetual ownership of real estate by institutions, such as churches. *Mortmain* literally means *mortus manus*—dead hand in Latin. Which is what your hand feels like when you sign a mortgage.

On the House

House and *dwelling* come from the Old English words *hus* and *dwellen*, respectively, but the most interesting words for the buildings we live in were imported from other languages. *Mansion* derives from the Latin *manere* (to remain, thus to dwell), which produced the Latin *mansio* (house). Today, *mansion* denotes a large, elaborate home, but it originally meant simply a place to live, be it ever so humble.

The word *palace* derives from the Palatine hill in Rome, where wealthy emperors like Augustus, Tiberius and Nero built huge mansions. These trophy villas were called *palatia*, which became *palais* in French and *palace* in English. By contrast, the small house known as a *bungalow* takes its name from the city of Bengal in India. *Bungalow* comes from the Hindustani word *bangla*, meaning of Bengal, and originally referred to the small house with a wide porch characteristic of architecture in eastern India.

The definition of *pavilion*—which can mean anything from a large tent, to an ornamental roofed structure, to a huge structure for expositions or sports events—is as elusive as a butterfly. And that's appropriate, for *pavilion* derives from the Latin word for a butterfly. In medieval France, large tents with their sides flapping in the wind reminded some people of butterflies, especially after these people had downed several bottles of wine. So such a structure was called a *paveillon*, based on the Latin *papilio*, butterfly.

Jerry's Kids

Pity poor Jerry. Or Gerry, for that matter. Thanks to the English language, men or women with these otherwise noble names are forever associated with slipshod construction or political manipulation.

If a house or machine or law is *jerry-built*, it's put together sloppily and carelessly. Remember the makeshift shelf in your uncle's garage supported on one end by his tackle box and on the other by an overturned flowerpot? Was you uncle, by any chance, named Jerry?

Language buffs have stumbled all over themselves trying to find the origin of *jerry-built*. A whole team of editors from the *Oxford English Dictionary* once swarmed over the headquarters of a British construction company reputed to do shoddy work, thinking they might find the source of the term. But they left empty-handed just before the office collapsed.

Other etymologists have speculated that *jerry* is short-hand for *Jericho* with its tumbling-down walls. Still others believe it comes from the French root *jour* (day), suggesting something poorly made might only stand for a day. The most likely explanation is that *jerry-built* is an adaptation of *jury- rigged*, a nautical term for a temporary or emergency arrangement of a ship's sails. This takes our hapless Uncle Jerry off the hook but leads to confusion with rigged juries, those courtroom panels preselected to be partial to one side or the other.

Called on the Carpet

Before reading this section, I want you to sit back in your favorite chair at home, take off your shoes and fall asleep . . . Hey, wait a minute!

If you enjoy sitting back and relaxing in your residence, you're exemplifying the original meaning of the word *residence*. For this word comes from the Latin *resideo*, a combination of *re-* (back) and *sedeo* (sit). As you sink your toes into that lush carpet, you should know that the word *carpet* derives from the Latin verb *carpo*, which meant to pluck. The first carpets were made of plucked or carded wool, and the name stuck to the rug—to say nothing of chewing gum. The Latin *carpo*, by the way, also lies at the feet of *excerpt* (something plucked out), *scarce* (something plucked over) and *carpe diem* (literally, pluck the day).

Now that you're comfortable, you might enjoy the view out a *bay window*. It's so called, not because it affords a good panorama of the harbor, but because the rectangular or semi-circular recess it provides reminded people of a tiny harbor or bay. (This term has also come to describe the not-so-tiny harbor that forms around the waist of a person who spends too much time exemplifying the original meaning of *residence*.)

That bay window is likely to have several *panes*, a word derived from the Latin *pannus*, meaning cloth or a piece of cloth. "Cloth isn't transparent!" you might protest. But once I tell you *pannus* also came to mean a piece of something, as in a piece of a window, the connection becomes transparent.

Those panes may afford a view of your *yard* and perhaps your *garden*. Both words, as it turns out, are derived from the Old English *geard*, meaning an enclosure. (Anyone who tells you *yard*, meaning distance, also comes from *geard* has three left feet. It descends from the Old High German *gart*, meaning a stick.) And, if your home is really bucolic, your view might include a barn. *Barn* is a blend of two Old English words—*bere* (barley) and *ærn* (place) because it was originally a place where farmers stored barley. Speaking of barley, this might be the perfect time for a tall, cold one. Hop to it!

STAR-SPANGLED BANTER
Words from the Natural World

Ever since Adam and Eve gave names to the plants and animals around them, we humans have felt an irresistible urge to label every natural object—from stars to storms to sturgeons. Whether it's a *blizzard* (from a slang word for a punch), a *comet* (from the Greek word for hair because its tail resembles tresses) or a *daisy* (from *day's eye*), our appellation trail has been out of this world.

Star Struck

Did you know the words *disaster, desire* and *consider* are all derived from Greek or Latin words for *star*? The Greek root *astron*, for instance, gives us *astronaut* (literally, star sailor), *astronomy* (star laws) and *astrology* (star discourse). *Astron* even blooms in *aster*, a flower with star-shaped petals. Because the ancients believed stars guided their destinies, a catastrophe was called a *disaster* (literally, away from the stars).

One of the Latin words for star was *stella*, a root that appears in *constellation* (formation of stars) and *stellar* (starlike). Another Latin word for star, *sidus*, appears in the Latin word *desiderare*, which meant to wish the stars would bring a favorable event. This sense of yearning for something survives in our English word *desire*.

Sidus also appears in the Latin word *considerare*, meaning the thoughtful examination of stars for clues to the future. *Consider*, which now means to study carefully, still retains this ponder–the-yonder connotation.

Even *influenza*, our word for a common viral infection, is star-struck. Up until the fifteenth century, the Italian word *influenza* meant the same thing as the English *influence*. But, when epidemics of disease plagued Europe during the 1400s, these outbreaks were blamed on the *influenza* of the stars, and soon the disease itself came to be called *influenza*, and the original meaning of *influenza* "flu" the coop.

Shady Characters

What does an eclipse of the moon have to do with umbrellas, peninsulas and ducks? Only the shadow knows. When a lunar eclipse occurs, the moon is first covered by the outer portion of the Earth's shadow known as the *penumbra*. Later, it enters the Earth's *umbra*, the much darker center of the Earth's shadow.

Umbra, the Latin word for shadow, gives us the word *umbrella* for the device that affords a welcome shadow of protection from rain or sun, as well as *umbrage*, which in addition to denoting shade or something that provides shade, means offense or resentment. ("The astronomer took umbrage at his students' indifference to the lunar eclipse.")

The linguistic link between *umbra* and *umbrage* is, appropriately enough, a bit shady. *Umbrage* probably evolved from the fact that, like the moon during an eclipse, the mood of an offended person visibly darkens. In fact, we describe a person who is easily offended as *umbrageous*. (Call a person who's easily offended a big word like that and you'll *really* be in trouble.)

Penumbra is a combination of the Latin word *paene*, meaning almost. Thus, a penumbra is almost a shadow. We sometimes use *penumbra* metaphorically to mean a gray area or a place where something exists to a lesser or uncertain degree. *Penumbra* can also refer to a vague doubt or suspicion. ("The candidate was tainted by the penumbra of impropriety.")

Other words using the prefix *pen-* to mean almost include the adjective *penultimate* (noun form *penult*), which means the next-to-last (or almost ultimate) item in a series, and *peninsula*, which literally means almost an island.

Eclipse comes from the Greek words *ek* (out) and *leipein* (to leave). So when something is eclipsed, it is left out or overshadowed, either literally or metaphorically. That's why the dull or colorless plumage that replaces the bright feathers of male ducks when breeding season ends is called *eclipse plumage*.

Earthy Language

In the beginning there was . . . "Chaos."

That's what the ancient Greeks called the swirling, transparent vapor they thought existed in the universe before any objects were formed. The confusion and disorder of the early universe abide in the meaning of our modern word "chaos," as well as in the words "mites' soccer game."

Another descendent of "chaos" is "gas." When Jan Baptista van Helmont, a Flemish chemist (try saying those two words a couple of times!), observed the vapors produced by burning charcoal (presumably while barbecuing), he decided to call these formless, amorphous substances "chaos." But he spelled "chaos" the way it was pronounced in Flemish, giving his former English teachers and the whole world "gas."

The Greeks believed that "Chaos" eventually took on an organized shape and form they called "Cosmos," their word for order, good arrangement. We still refer to the universe as the "cosmos," and this root survives in "cosmic" (vast, significant), "cosmopolitan" (worldly), "microcosm" (small world) and "cosmetic" (something that brings order to chaos and, in the case of cosmetic surgery, order to Kay).

According to Greek myth, the first gods to emerge from Chaos were Ouranos and Gaia. Think of this pair as Woody Allen and Diane Keaton in the movie Annie Hall. Ouranos was the wild, zany god of the sky, while Gaia was the down-to-earth goddess of the earth.

Earth mother Gaia's name survives in English as a prefix for many words related to our planet—"geography" (description of the earth), "geology" ("science of the earth") and "geometry" (measurement of the earth while simultaneously torturing high-school sophomores).

The Romans gave the Greek goddess Gaia two names— "Terra" and "Tellus." Terra has its feet planted firmly in many earthy English words—"terrace," "territory," "terrain," "terraruim," "extra-terrestrial," "terra cotta" (cooked earth), even "terrier" (ground dog).

But "tellus" is the "terra incognita" of earth words. It survives only in a few English words you've probably never heard of.

"Please tell us!" you say? Well, OK—"tellurian" (of or relating to the earth), "tellurion" (an apparatus that depicts the movement of the earth on its axis and around the sun) and "tellurium" (a brittle, silvery white metallic element).

As for good old "earth," this word comes from the Old English "eaorthe," a descendent of the Germanic "ertho," meaning—what else?—earth.

Stars of Wander

When the ancient Greeks looked up at the night skies, they noticed that some of the "stars" seemed to wander from place to place each night against the backdrop of the fixed stars. They called these bodies *planetes* after their word *planasthai*, meaning to wander.

We now know, of course, that these planets are not stars at all but our close companions in the solar system. Viewed from Earth, they appear to move erratically because they and the Earth are constantly changing their relative positions as they revolve around the sun.

The ancient Greeks, and later the Romans, were so fascinated with these celestial ramblers that they named each one after a god who shares its attributes in some way.

Mercury—Because Mercury is the closest planet to the sun, it appears to move faster than any of the others. Thus, the Greeks named it after Hermes, the winged-footed messenger of the gods. The Romans changed Hermes' name to Mercury, and we still call someone whose mood changes quickly *mercurial* (along with a lot of other names we can't repeat here.)

The Romans gave Mercury's name to a silvery metal that moved almost as fast as he did: *argentum vivum*, literally living silver, now known as *quicksilver* or, in cold climates where the plunging mercury requires warm clothing, "long-john silver."

Today Mercury is often depicted as a slim, handsome youth, with a winged hat and sandals. FTD, the floral delivery service that uses Mercury as its symbol, found the perfect person to represent this dewy-cheeked Adonis: the bearded, burly former NFL lineman Merlin Olsen.

(By the way, do you know what "FTD" stands for?)

Mercury also entered our language in a more indirect way. Mercury's Greek name was *Hermes*, and the Greeks identified Hermes with Thoth, the Egyptian god of wisdom.

Finding they couldn't pronounce Thoth unless they had ingested huge quantities of ouzo, the Greeks called him "Thrice-Great Hermes" or "Hermes Trismegistos" which nobody could pronounce, drunk or sober.

(Is it "Flowers That Droop"? Nope.)

Anyway, the Greeks and Romans believed Hermes Trismegistos had invented a magic seal to keep bottles and other vessels airtight. So, from this invention of Hermes came the English word *hermetic*, meaning completely sealed from outside air or influence, or, metaphorically, Michael Jackson.

(It's "Florists Transworld Delivery.")

Venus—The second-closest planet to the sun and the planet nearest to Earth seemed brighter and more beautiful than any star. The Greeks paid tribute to its loveliness by naming it after Aphrodite, their good-looking goddess of love. The Romans called Aphrodite *Venus*, and we still describe someone we love and respect as *venerable*.

Mars—The Greek god of war was Ares, so it seemed logical to name the planet that had a reddish, bloody hue after him. *Ares* became *Mars* under the Romans, and today we use the word *martial* to describe someone or something with warlike qualities, as in *martial law*.

Jupiter—Because one planet was almost as bright as Venus and, unlike Venus, often shone all night, the Greeks named it for their chief god, Zeus. Under the Romans, *Zeus* became *Jupiter*.

Saturn—In ancient times, before the planets Uranus, Neptune and Pluto had been discovered, the Greeks named the slowest-moving planet after their god of time, Cronus, who had previously done time as their god of farming. When the Romans adopted Cronus, they renamed him and his plodding planet *Saturn*. Saturn's heavy, sluggish quality is reflected in our word *saturnine*, meaning sad, sullen.

Uranus—When the German-born British astronomer William Herschel discovered this distant planet in 1781, he wanted to call it "Georgium Sidus" ("the Georgian Planet") in honor of King George III. The King had recently lost the American colonies, and perhaps Herschel assumed his highness needed some consolation—or at least a constellation.

But others sided against "Georgium Sidus." After all, they reasoned, each of the other planets had been named for a Roman or Greek god, which George III was definitely not. So the German astronomer Johann Bode suggested the name "Uranus," the Roman spelling of the Greek god of the sky, "Ouranos."

This choice boded well because the god Uranus was also the father of Saturn (Uranus' neighboring planet), and Saturn, in turn, was the father of Jupiter (Saturn's neighboring planet). This created a nice little three-generation succession in the middle of the solar system, not unlike Britain's: George I ("Onesy"), George II ("Dubbya") and George III ("Trippya").

Eight years after Herschel scoped out Uranus, the German chemist Martin Heinrich Klaproth discovered a new metal. "Eureka!" he shouted. "On second thought, Uranus!" Klaproth named the metal "uranium" in honor of the recently discovered planet.

Uranus has at least twenty moons, which brings up the issue of how to pronounce "Uranus." The preferred, polite-company rendering is "YOOR-ah-nus," but, to the delight of sophomores everywhere, "yoor-AY-nus" is also acceptable.

Neptune—During the 1800s, astronomers still giggling over the latter pronunciation of "Uranus," noticed that Uranus was orbiting a bit more slowly than their calculations had predicted. Something must be dragging it down.

After ruling out friction, wind resistance and heavy chains, they concluded that the culprit must be the gravitational pull of an unseen planet. So in 1846 they pointed their telescopes at the place where such a planet should be only to discover—Bingo!—Marlon Brando.

Actually, they discovered Neptune, which they named for the Roman god of the sea simply because he was Jupiter's brother and lacked his own planet. It was a combination of nepotism and opportunism. Call it neptunism.

Pluto—Both scientifically and linguistically, Pluto is a misfit. Much smaller and rockier than the other outer planets, it spins more slowly than they do and, like a ninth-rate restaurant, has almost no atmosphere.

Befitting its rogue status, Pluto is the only planet (other than Earth) named for a Greek god rather than a Roman one. Because it moves through darkness, far away from the sun's light, it was given the name of Pluto, the Greek god of Hades, the murky underworld. And, appropriately enough, Pluto's small moon Charon is named for the grim ferryman who transported souls over the river Styx to Hades.

The astronomers who discovered Pluto in 1931 could have named it after the Roman god of the underworld, Father Dis, but they dissed *Dis* in favor of *Pluto*. (Some say they were influenced by the canine character who had recently appeared in Walt Disney's first animated cartoons, but this Mickey Mouse explanation strikes some experts as goofy.)

Others say *Pluto* was chosen because its first two letters honor Percy Lowell, the American astronomer who spent many years searching for Pluto without success. Initially, this made sense, and it certainly pleased loyal adherents of the Percy faith. Nine years after Pluto was detected, scientists discovered two new radioactive elements. Because these elements follow uranium on the periodic table, in the same way

Neptune and Pluto follow Uranus in the solar system, these new substances were named *neptunium* and *plutonium*.

Since there's no life on Pluto, it doesn't have a *plutocracy* (a wealthy class that controls the government). But there's an interesting connection between the planet Pluto and riches. Because precious metals, like gold and silver, come from the underworld ruled by Pluto, the Greek word for wealth is *ploutos*, a root that gives our language *plutocracy*. Isn't that rich?

Words Carved in Stone

The origins of some words are only a stone's throw away. The ancient Romans, for instance, noticed that a troublesome ethical issue irritates the soul the way a tiny pebble in the shoe irritates the sole. After a long march, a Roman legionary could often pick enough stones from his shoes to make an abacus (and a soldier cuss). So eventually, the Latin word for a small, sharp stone (*scrupulus*) also came to mean any source of anxiety or worry. That's why, in English, a *scruple* is an ethical consideration or principle that, like a stone in the shoe, tends to inhibit action.

Calculate has also traveled a long and rocky road to its present meaning. In Latin, a *calx* was a pebble used as a counting piece in games and reckoning. This stone meaning of *calx* soon calcified in English as *calcium*, *calcite* and *calculus* (an accretion in the body, such as a kidney stone). In passing (ouch!), I'll mention that the rolling *calx* even gathered enough semantic moss to give us *calculate* and *calculus* (a field of mathematics).

Also mined in the Roman quarry is *dilapidated* (literally, to have stones missing from). Stone-faced purists claim the meaning of *dilapidated* has become dilapidated in recent decades. These rock-ribbed hard-liners say *dilapidated* should be used only to describe structures made of stone, such as Stonehenge, the Colosseum and their own hearts. It's wrong, they say, to speak of a "dilapidated house," a "dilapidated car" or a "dilapidated usage rule," unless these objects are made of stone (or, in the case of the usage rule, carved in stone).

In fact, the English word *dilapidate* comes not directly from the Latin *lapis* but from *dilapidatus*, which even in Roman times was a general term for *destroyed*. So the dilapidated dinosaurs who insist that *dilapidated* be used only for objects made of stone are living in the Stone Age.

Stop and Spell the Flowers

"Say it with flowers," the florists tell us, and indeed, the names given to many common flowers say some surprising things about both botanical and linguistic history. *Daisy*, for instance, comes from the phrase "day's eye." That's because, like the human eye, a daisy opens when the sun comes up and closes at dusk, unless there's something good on TV that night.

The *dandelion* derives its name, not from its yellow-maned flower, but from its jagged-edged leaves, which the French called *dent de lion* (teeth of the lion). So when the Cowardly Lion in *The Wizard of Oz* boasts that he's not a "dandy lion," he's actually lying through his teeth.

Impatiens are so called because their ripe pods burst open impatiently as soon as they are touched. *Asters* are named for their resemblance to stars, while the multi-hued iris comes from the Greek word for rainbow. The flowery vine known as the *passionflower* was so christened, not because it inspired romantic love, but because parts of it resemble the cross on which the Passion of Christ occurred.

Small round flowers with jagged petals are often called *bachelor buttons*. That's because, in the old days, the cloth buttons of wifeless, helpless men were often frayed around the edges, to say nothing of the men themselves. The *nasturtium* is named after the pungent odor of its juice. In Latin, its name is *nasus* (nose) and *tortare* (to twist), thus literally nose-twisting.

Tulips, which were imported to Europe from the Middle East and seemed to resemble turbans in their shape, were named after *tülbend*, the Turkish word for the gauze that wraps turbans. Likewise, the *delphinium* is so named because the gland that secretes that flower's nectar is shaped like a dolphin (the mammal, not the fish). *Carnations* come in many colors, but the pink ones resembled the skin of Caucasians, so they were named after the Latin root for flesh, *carn*.

Other flowery prose includes:

peony—In Greek mythology, Paion was the physician to the gods. He would zip furiously around Mt. Olympus, healing Achilles' heel and pandering to Pan's pains, but always taking Wednesday afternoon off for golf. So when the Greeks discovered that a certain large-flowered plant could be used for medicinal purposes, they named it *peony* for Paion.

gladiolus—The glads that make us glad are named for, of all things, their sword-shaped leaves. *Gladiolus* comes from the Latin *gladius* (sword), the same root that gives us *gladiator*. But there's absolutely no truth to the rumor that bloodthirsty Romans gave gladiators the green thumbs-down sign.

foxglove—This herb is so named because its tubular flowers resemble the empty finger of a glove. The Latin name for foxglove is *digitalis*, meaning of a finger. That's why the powerful cardiac stimulant made from the dried powdered leaf of the foxglove is called *digitalis*. (Alas, the origin of this word's first syllable has outfoxed scholars.)

hydrangea—The seed capsules of these large-flowered plants reminded someone of small water jars. Thus, *hydrangea* is a combination of two Greek roots: *hydr-* (water) and *angeion* (vessel, container). (*Angeion*, meaning blood vessel, is also the root of *angiogram*, an X-ray of the blood vessels.)

pansy—To some eyes, the velvety little faces of pansy flowers look pensive and thoughtful. Thus, pansies are thoughtfully named after the Old French *pensee* (thought, remembrance), the same root that gives us *pensive*.

azalea—The name of this flowering shrub derives from the Greek *azaleos*, dry. Some say azaleas are so named because they thrive in dry soil; others say it's because the texture of their wood is dry. Talk about a dry discussion!

geranium—Someone, perhaps after a bit too much wine, thought the seed pod of this plant resembled the bill of a crane, so its name derives from the Greek *geranos*, crane. In fact, another name for geranium is *cranesbill*. When it comes to geraniums, the bird is the word.

Nic' Names

(Note: the Surgeon General has determined that reading this section may be hazardous to your health).

Tobacco is a Spanish word. It may come from the Caribbean Indian word for the device used to inhale tobacco, or perhaps from the Arabic *tabbâc*, meaning bad stuff people get hooked on. King James I of England called tobacco *sotweed*, apparently because people who smoked it became sotted, that is, stupefied or muddled.

Nicotine, the active ingredient in tobacco, was named for Jean Nicot, a sixteenth-century French diplomat who, while ambassador to Portugal, received some American tobacco from a Belgian merchant. When Nicot presented the tobacco to his sovereign, the notorious Catherine de Medici, she was so impressed with its Medici-nal effects that she dubbed tobacco *Nicotiane* in his honor and ordered five more cartons.

The cigarette brand name *Lucky Strike* was first used for plug tobacco popular among miners seeking lucky strikes in the gold and silver fields of the Far West. The dromedary pictured on Camel packs is the beloved Barnum and Bailey circus camel Old Joe, which is why the brand's controversial mascot is still called "Joe Camel" today. The famous expression "What this country needs is a good five-cent cigar" was coined when Vice President Thomas R. Marshall threw his two cents into a Senate debate over the country's needs during Woodrow Wilson's administration.

A *panatela*, a thin, straight cigar about five inches long, is named for its resemblance to a long, thin biscuit, called a *panatella* in Spanish, from the Latin *panis* (bread), which may explain why people like to smoke panatelas while loafing.

Stogy, which now refers to any strong, cheap cigar, is an abbreviation of *Conestoga*, the name of the southeastern Pennsylvania town famous for producing two products: covered wagons and a torpedo-shaped cigars. Appropriately enough, the Conestoga cigar was a favorite of Conestoga wagon drivers, who thought its foul smell might repel Indians. (It didn't; see expression "circle the wagons.") The Conestoga, which grew shorter in length as it was smoked, also grew shorter in name, becoming *stogy* (or *stogie*).

(Before you snuff out that butt, here's a linguistic "left"-over: Conestoga wagons, for some unknown reason, were built with their brakes on the left-hand side, forcing their drivers to sit on the left. So, in order to have a full view of the road, the drivers drove on the right side of the road. As Bill Bryson points out in his delightful book *Made in America*, this quirk of Conestoga wagons was apparently what started the American practice of driving on the right instead of the left, where British drivers are "left"-tenants.)

Divine Comety

The word *comet* comes from, of all things, the resemblance of its long, streaking tail to human hair. It was none other than Aristotle who first used the Greek word *kometes*, meaning wearing long hair, to describe these wondrous filaments of the firmament.

One question that comes around whenever a comet comes around is whether the *Halley* of Halley's comet is pronounced "HAY-lee," (as in Hayley Mills) or "HAL-ee" (rhymes with *alley*). Sorry, Hayley (though your performance in *The Moonspinners* was out of this world). It's "HAL-ee," after the English astronomer Edmund Halley.

Comets, of course, are not to be confused with meteoroids, which are small, solid objects hurtling through space. But did you know that *meteoroid, meteor* and *meteorite* have slightly different meanings? A meteoroid becomes a meteor when it's heated to incandescence by friction with the Earth's atmosphere and creates a bright trail or streak. If the meteoroid does not burn up completely and falls to Earth, it becomes a meteorite.

The Bird Is the Word

The Latin word for bird, *avis*, still soars quite plainly in several English terms—*aviary*, *avian* and *aviation*, as well as *rara avis*, literally meaning rare bird and, metaphorically, any rarity. (True slogan of Avis Rent-a-Car: "We fly harder.")

But the Latin word *avis* flies below the radar in *bustard* and *ostrich*. *Bustard*, denoting a game bird found in Europe, Asia, Africa and Australia, derives ultimately from the Latin *avis tarda*, slow bird, which this large game bird tends to be. *Avis tarda* became *bistarde* in Middle French and *bustard* in English. (*Buzzard*, by the way, which you might assume buzzes in from *bustard*, actually comes from the Latin word for hawk—*buteon*.)

In the case of *ostrich*, the Latin *avis* has stuck its head even deeper into the sand. *Ostrich* derives from the French *ostrusce*, which itself comes from the Latin term *avis struthio*, literally, bird ostrich.

A Latin stump form of *avis* was *auspex*, meaning someone who foretold the future from the behavior of birds. (Today we call such a person a stock analyst.) *Auspex* gives us *auspicious*, meaning propitious, favorable. And, because a soothsayer was an influential person, *auspex* expanded to mean a patron or supporter, giving us *auspices*, sponsorship.

By contrast, *pigeon* comes not from any fancy Latin words but from the sounds it makes. The Romans called any young bird a *pipio* in imitation of its sharp piping cries. *Pipio* became *pijon* in French and *pigeon* in English, denoting a specific type of bird with a stout body, short legs, smooth, compact plumage and an alarming affinity for statues. But pigeons, you might object, don't pipe; they coo. True, but their young make high-pitched piping sounds when hungry. Hence, *pipio* and *pijon* came to denote the entire breed, both young and old.

Other birds whose names imitate the sounds of their calls include the bobolink, bobwhite, cuckoo, chickadee, cock (from "cock-a-doodle-doo") and whippoorwill, which, if you've ever had one sit and sing on your roof all night, as I have, is sometimes called "a little bustard"—or words to that effect.

Reasons for the Seasons

To everything there is a season and to every season there is a word. But where do the words for the four seasons come from?

To find the source of *spring*, you surely don't need a divining Rob. As you might suspect, spring springs from *spring*, meaning to rise or leap, because so many things spring up during this season—flowers, grass, IRS deadlines, lawnmower repair bills. (Given this reasoning, we're lucky that winter and summer aren't called "shake" and "bake," respectively.)

The English *summer* is closely related to the German *Sommer*, especially when a hot, humid air mass extends from Berlin to London. In fact, *summer* simmers all the way back to the Sanskrit word *rama*, which means season or year, and we still occasionally use, *summer* to mean year, as in, "She was a lass of thirteen summers."

But if that lass performs a somersault in July, it has nothing to do with summer, or, alas, even salt. *Somersault* is a rollover from the Old French *sombresaut*, which flipped in from the Latin *salt*, meaning leap, as it does in *assault*, *sally*, and *Salientia* (the biological category for leaping frogs and toads).

Like *spring*, *fall* refers to a general direction of vegetative movement. In fact, its full name was once "faul of the leafe," but mouthing all this was such a downer that it was soon shortened to *fall*. Interestingly, the use of *fall* for autumn took a leaf of absence from Great Britain. Common in England until the 1800s, it died out there but still survives in the United States. *Autumn*, although it descends from the Latin word for fall (*autumnus*), is not linked to the Fall of Rome.

Winter is indeed an old man, dating all the way back to the Indo-European root *wed*, meaning either wet or white, depending on your climate. *Wed* gave us the German *wintruz* (wet season) which drained into English as *winter*.

But why do people *summer* in Maine and *winter* in Florida, but never *spring* or *fall* anywhere? Likewise, why do we *summerize* and *winterize* our cars, but never *springize* or *autumnize* our gardens? Call it "seasonal inflection disorder."

You've Said a Mouthful

Words of Food and Drink

English has often been compared to a lavish banquet, replete with plump adjectives, juicy verbs and spicy adverbs. Its tasty nouns for food and drink are no exception. Whether you're a vegetarian (from the Latin *vegetabilis*, meaning life-giving or animated) or a carnivore (from the Latin *carnis*, meaning flesh), you'll find plenty of food for discussion.

Salty Language

The English language is peppered with salt. *Salt* is not only in your *salad*, *sauce* and *sausage*, but in your *salary* as well. (Warning: If you're on a low-salt diet, stop reading now.)

In Roman times, when salt was a precious food preservative, soldiers were actually paid in salt. ("No salt, no assault!" shouted the legionnaires when they struck for higher pay.) This payment, called a *salarium* in Latin, eventually became *salary* in English, and it's what keeps most of us going back to the salt mines everyday. You might think the phrase "worth your salt" derives from these salty salaries. Nope. Here's the saline solution: it comes from the salty beef, called *salt*, eaten by sailors. When an old salt's salad days were long over, he was said to be "not worth his salt."

And speaking of *salad*, the Romans seasoned their dishes of lettuce and other raw vegetables so heavily with salt (*sal* in Latin) that the dishes themselves came to be called *salata*. After being tossed from Portugal to France, *salata* finally landed in England as *salad*.

Salt is also a mover and shaker in *sauce, salsa* and *sausage* (because they contain so much you-know-what). And, to make a long sausage short, *salt* is ingrained in *salami,* too. And when Jesus called his disciples the "salt of the earth," they took it as a compliment, not a condiment. He didn't mean they were zesty or spicy; He meant they were as precious as salt.

Of course, you should take everything you hear about salt with a grain of salt—including the origin of the phrase "with a grain of salt." While some will tell you it comes from the Latin phrase *cum grano salis,* don't believe it. This Latin phrase was actually concocted long *after* the English saying became as common as table salt. The expression suggests that questionable statements, like tainted meat, can only be swallowed with enough salt to cover their foul taste.

And now for the last leg of our sodium chlor-ride. If you've ever asked someone to "pass you the salt cellar," you're guilty of double salting. *Cellar* (from the French *salar*) originally meant salt in English. But people confused *cellar,* meaning salt, with its homograph *cellar,* meaning a place for storage. So when you ask for the "salt cellar," you're technically asking for the salt salt.

Counter Intuitive

"Wreck a pair, burn the British, draw a midnight with sugar, and squeeze one!" When the waitress in your favorite diner shouts these short orders to the cook, you'll have your breakfast in short order: two scrambled eggs, English muffins, black coffee with sugar, and orange juice.

You won't hear jive like that in today's "Hi-my-name-is-Steve-and-I'll-be-your-server" joints, but hashslingers' lingo still sings and sizzles in down-home eateries across the land. With the help of slanguist Stuart Berg Flexner and my friends at the Quaker Diner in West Hartford, Connecticut, where I was once a "reglah," here's a short stack of pancake poetry.

Not surprisingly, a lot of diner jargon has its genesis in the Garden of Eatin'. "Adam and Eve on a raft," for egg-sample, is two poached eggs on toast; "Eve with the lid on" is apple pie (Eve's forbidden fruit); "Adam's Ale" is water; a "first lady" is spareribs (borrowed from Adam); and "Noah's boy" is a slice of ham (Noah's second son).

Diner talk tells it like it is, and often, as it was. Beef stew is "bossy in a bowl," a hot dog is a "ground hog," ham on rye is "pig on whiskey," and meat cooked rare is "on the hoof."

Ordering! "Burn one!" Cook a hamburger. "Burn a pup!" Grill a hot dog. "Burn the van!" Mix a vanilla malt. "Customer wants to take a chance!" Serve up the hash. You don't want ice? "Hold the hail!" No butter? "High and dry!" No lettuce? "Keep off the grass!"

Pick a number: "5" (glass of milk); "41" (lemonade); "51" (hot chocolate, a.k.a. "ha cha"); "55" (root beer); "81" (a glass of water, a.k.a. "on the city"); "86" (we're out of it, or that patron is out of it, i.e., broke or drunk); "87" (check out the good-looker who just entered); "95" (that customer is leaving without paying); "99" (be on your toes—the boss is here).

So the next time you order a tuna salad sandwich on toast at your favorite diner, see if the waitress or waiter broadcasts this: "Radio!" (Anything toasted is "down," so a "tuna down," as in "tune it down," is a "radio.") Isn't it too bad that this well-done linguistic medium is increasingly rare?

Spirited Discussions

At closing time in medieval German beer gardens, the bartender would call, *"Gar aus!* (all out!)."* Whether this meant all of you get out or we're all out of beer is uncertain, but the message was clear: Scram! When English visitors heard the term *gar aus*, they imported it (along with many kegs of German beer) into their own country. Soon anyone who stayed at a bar till *gar aus* time was said to be *garausing*, which eventually became *carousing*.

By contrast, English bartenders often dispersed carousers in pubs with the ever-so-polite call, "Hurry up, please, it's time!" a phrase immortalized in T.S. Eliot's classic poem about kicked-out customers, "The Chased Land."

Let's continue our bibulous explorations:

toast—Some British etymologists believe raising a glass to honor someone is called a *toast* because spiced toast crumbs were once sprinkled into drinks to flavor them. But other experts say this is just another example of the English muffin' a word origin, and that this bread-based theory is *toast* (today's trendy word for burned up, wrecked, destroyed).

grog—This term for rum diluted with water (what, in my impoverished scholar days, I called a "graduate school martini") is named for the eighteenth-century British admiral Edward Vernon. Because Admiral Vernon often decked himself out in a cloak made of a coarse silk fabric called *grogram*, his sailors nicknamed him "Old Grog."

One day, under the cloak of secrecy, Old Grog watered down his sailors' daily ration of rum. The sailors (who were now ir-rational, in more ways than one) suspected something was wrong but couldn't find proof; in fact, that's just what they wanted—more proof. Soon, they sarcastically dubbed the low-alcohol rum *grog*, and we still call people who act as if they've had too much grog "graduate students."

Slurred Speech

Which human endeavor has inspired the highest number of colorful phrases in English?

    a) accounting   b) coin collecting
    c) golfing   d) drinking.

You guessed it. Scholars have recorded over two thousand terms for inebriation alone, a lush supply indeed, especially considering most people don't drink alone. Not surprisingly, many of these terms begin with the letter *sh . . . er . . . s*: *stewed, soused, stiffed, stinking, snuffy, sozzled, spiflicated, shellacked, sloshed, smashed, schnockered, sauced*—and those are just the ones we can print in this book.

The origins of other terms can be equally intoxicating:

three sheets in the wind—This is, indeed, a nautical term, but the sheets referred to are not sails. They're the ropes or chains attached to the lower corner of a sail to control its angle. When one sheet is loosened, the sail flaps in the wind and the ship loses power. But if three sheets are in the wind, the ship lurches out of control, reeling like a drunk.

half seas over—This expression has two explanations, both foamy: 1) The tipsy gait of an intoxicated person resembles a ship heeled over in the wind, with its deck half awash. So a person so impaired is said, like the ship, to be *half-seas over*. 2) The term may be an English rendering of the Dutch *op ze zober* (oversea beer), a particularly potent brew imported to England from the Netherlands. So a Brit who drank too much *op ze zober* was said to be *half seas over*.

lush—This origin of this term for a heavy drinker has inspired many barroom brawls. On one side are those who bellow, "This term is eponyminish, er . . . eponymononish, er . . . eponyminniemouse . . . the heck with it . . . it's derived from someone's name." Indeed, Dr. Thomas Lushington (1590–1661) was an English chaplain who liked drinking so much that a London drinking club was named "The City of Lushington" in his honor.

But the problem is that no one can prove the word *lush* derives from "The City of Lushington." It may simply be that *lush*, with its sloppy, slurry *sh* sound and link with luscious indulgence, came to mean drunkard all on its own.

Meaty Misteak

I hate to pick a beef with one of the most respected foreign correspondents in network TV news, but Mark Phillips of CBS once butchered the derivation of *sirloin*. Reporting on Britain's mad cow disease, Phillips noted that Brits love their beef so much that they once went so far as to knight a particularly fine cut "Sir Loin," giving us the word *sirloin*. Unfortunately, this widely accepted etymology, as juicy and tasty as it is, is a misteak.

One man's meat is another man's métier, and the authoritative linguist Hugh Rawson outflanks this benighted beknighted legend in his authoritative book *Devious Derivations*. Rawson explains that *sirloin*, like many other

English words related to cooking, comes from a French word. In this case it's *surlonge* (*sur*, meaning over, above, and *longe*, meaning loin).

Not surprisingly, the British associated the French prefix *sur* with the English title *sir*, and soon they were sir-ving dinners featuring "Sir Loyne of Beef," convening the "Knights of the Top Round Table" and assembling noblemen for "rump parliaments."

The English even cooked up several theories about which king first knighted the beef. Leading candidates included Henry "Prime Cut" VIII, James "Medium Rare" I and Charles "Ground Chuck" II. So popular was the "Sir Loyne" misconception, in fact, that two sirloins joined at the backbone were given the exalted title "baron of beef," while the larders of commoners remained barren of beef.

Eat-ymologies

If you've ever wondered who Betty Crocker is, what the two Ms in "M&M" stand for, or whether it's *ketchup* or *catsup*, here's a cook's *tour de farce*.

The name of the fictional cookster *Betty Crocker* honors a company director named William Crocker. *Sara Lee* comes from Sara Lee Schupf, daughter of the bakery's founder. *Birds Eye* frozen foods are named, not for feathery field filchers, but for firm-founder Charles Birdseye. *M&M* comes literally from Mars: the last names of Frank Mars, founder of Mars candy, and Bob Murrie, company president in 1941.

Spam is short for *spiced ham*; *Velveeta* means velvety cheese; *Tab* helps you keep tab of your weight, and the exotic *Häagen-Dazs* was simply made up by the wife of a Bronx ice-cream maker. Likewise, *7 UP*, originally called "Bib-label Lithiated Lemon-Lime Soda," was christened by default after its inventor rejected six other names.

When nutritionists began caning sugar in the 1980s, the makers of Sugar Crisp, Sugar Frosted Flakes and Sugar Smacks quietly changed the names of these cereals to *Golden Crisp*, *Frosted Flakes*, and *Smacks*, respectively, and almost no one noticed. But, when Coors renamed its Banquet Beer as *Coors Original Draft* in 1988, the company lost many long-time customers.

And, just in case you were wondering, *ketchup* won over *catsup* when Del Monte finally capitulated in 1988, and Yankee Doodle called his feather *macaroni* because *macaroni* was a then slang term for dandy.

But perhaps the most memorable food name is "Radiator Charlie's Mortgage Lifters." These were tomatoes so large and juicy that the West Virginia shade-tree mechanic who grew them paid off his mortgage with the proceeds.

Potluck Supper

In merry olde England, sportsmen followed very strict rules about what game animals could be hunted and when. Vigilant game wardens, wearing bright orange jump suits and lugging thick manuals full of regulations, patrolled the forests, looking for violators. But illiterate peasants, who simply wanted small pieces of meat for their stew pots, would often flout these rules by bagging animals out of season and killing immature animals.

Game warden to peasant: "Hey, it says here in subsection 26, paragraph 8, that you can't shoot that baby muskrat until the first mayfly is seen after St. Gregory's Day."

Peasant: "Sneck up, Govenuh! I needs some meats to put in me pot. Blam!"

Such illegal shots were called *pot shots*, and, eventually, any unfair or unsportsmanlike attack came to be called a *pot shot*.

If we stir this medieval stew pot again, we'll discover the origin of *potluck*. Though travelers stopping at the castles of nobles were sure to be offered a choice of many fine meats, visitors to commoners' cottages took their chances with whatever happened to be simmering in the stew pot: baby muskrats, mayflies, St. Gregory. So *potluck* came to mean whatever item is available at a given time.

Two other "pots" of speech are *potboiler* and *go to pot*. You might assume the term *potboiler*, meaning an inferior literary work, was derived from the fact that writers of second-rate adventure novels tried to keep their plots boiling along to sustain readers' interest. In fact, *potboilers* are so called because authors write them primarily for money—to keep their pots of food boiling.

Similarly, you might assume *go to pot*, meaning to come to ruin, referred to a plant's dying and falling back into its pot. In fact, this phrase is derived from the practice of throwing undesirable remnants of food into the stew pot. So anything that has degenerated or become inferior is said to have *gone to pot*.

Smorgas-word

A surprising number of foods and beverages take their names from geographic locations. The ancient Romans, for instance, imported the peach from Persia, so they called it *Persicum malum* (Persian apple). Eventually, *malum* was dropped, and *Persicum* became *péche* in French and *peach* in English. (Just how all this happened is a bit fuzzy.) Likewise, the Moroccan city of Tangier and the Greek cities of Corinth and Cerasus bore fruit in the names *tangerine*, *currant* and *cherry*, respectively.

O Porto, the main port of Portugal, is the port of call for *port* wine, while *sherry* hails from the Roman settlement Xeres in the Spanish province of Cadiz. Speaking of beverages, *seltzer* honors the Prussian village of Selters, known for its bubbling spring water and *bourbon* bears the name of the Kentucky county where this potent liquor is "still" made.

Cappuccino is on the lips (literally) of many people these days. The name of this trendy drink comes, not from a place, but from a garment. In 1525 a new order of Catholic monks was founded in Europe. Because each member wore a long, pointed cowl called a *cappuccino* (from the Italian word for hood), they became known as the *Capuchin* order. Later on, the name *Capuchin* was given to non-human monks—monkeys with tufts of black hair resembling tiny cowls (a cowl lick, you might say). Soon, any group of these unruly simians was called the Capuchin *dis*order.

Meanwhile, back in Italy, a blend of espresso coffee mixed with steamed milk was dubbed *cappuccino* because it was the same color as the habit worn by the Capuchin friars. So if you give up cappuccino for good, you'll literally be kicking the habit.

Whence *deviled eggs*? When explorers returned to Europe with the red pods of a shrub discovered in South America, chefs ground up these pods into a pepper and sprinkled it on a variety of chopped-up dishes. "Zowie, that's hot!" exclaimed the first tasters, and soon this fiery red pepper was being compared to hell and the devil. So any food sprinkled with a hot spice—from lamb to fish to eggs—was said to be *deviled*.

NAME GAME

The People behind the Words

$\mathcal{T}$he English language is well peopled with words derived from people. Such words are called *eponyms* (EP-uh-nims) from the Greek word meaning after a name. According to Hoyle, an eponym is technically the person's name, not the word derived from it, but only a *Scrooge* would insist on this *Draconian* distinction. The people behind some of these eponyms may keep you *mesmerized*.

Naming Names

berserk—Berserk was an ancient Scandinavian hero so fierce that he wore a bearskin shirt (*berserk*) instead of armor in battle. Ferocious warriors who followed his Norse code of warfare (shot, shot, slash) became known as *berserks*, and soon *berserk* came to mean deranged.

paparazzi—Pesky celebrity photographers are named for Paparazzo, a star-stalking shutterbug in Frederico's Fellini's 1960 film *La Dolce Vita*. Speaking of bugs, the etymology of *Paparazzo* comes from entomology. Fellini chose the word, he said, because it suggested a "buzzing, stinging, annoying sort of insect."

ritzy—Born a Swiss peasant, César Ritz went from rags to Ritzes. Starting as a waiter, he eventually became manager of London's elegant Savoy Hotel. Then, stomping on the Savoy, Ritz quit to build luxurious Ritz Hotels in Paris and London. Soon *ritzy* had checked into English, meaning fancy.

59

fudge—When people *fudge* (falsify) data, they may be imitating the dishonesty of a seventeenth-century sea captain known as "Lying Fudge." Captain Fudge was so deep in deep-sea deceit that *to fudge it* came to mean to lie. But some experts say this nautical derivation is itself a fudge, and claim that *fudge* comes from *fadge*, to fit.

maverick—During the 1830s, Samuel Augustus Maverick, a genteel eastern attorney who sported shiny shoes and fancy shirts, moved to Texas and started a law practice. When one of his clients couldn't pay in cash, Maverick accepted payment in land near San Antonio instead, where he soon established the Conquistar Ranch.

But Maverick was so preoccupied with fighting to win the independence of Texas from Mexico that he rarely visited his ranch. In his absence, his indolent ranch hands never got around to branding his calves. On the few occasions Maverick did visit, he would plaster yellow sticky notes all over the bunkhouse reading, "Remember to brand calves!" But even this didn't work. Soon Maverick's unbranded cattle were roaming all over Texas. Neighboring ranchers began calling these renegades "mavericks," and, within a few years, this term was being applied to human nonconformists.

charley horse—There are two possible origins of this term for an upper leg cramp, both equally lame. Some say it goes back to the reign of Charles II in England, when the partially disabled veterans given jobs as night watchmen were called *charleys* after the King. By somewhat extensive extension, lame horses became known as *charleys* and muscle cramps as *charley horses*.

Others say it's the legacy of Charley, a horse who pulled a roller for the Chicago White Sox grounds crew during the 1890s. Because Charley walked with a distinctive limp, he soon became a ballpark figure, so to speak, and baseball fans soon started calling any player suffering from muscular stiffness a *charley horse*. But in 1889, before Charley rolled, a Cincinnati newspaper described a ball player's injury as a *charley horse*, so it doesn't take a lot of horse sense to realize that somebody's pulling our leg.

let George do it—The George who was always ready to perform any task was Georges d'Amboise who, from 1498 to 1510, was the right-hand man for France's King Louis XII. Georges was right handy at what he did, too, earning his boss's acclaim by reforming the tax code and the court system. In fact, it became a standing joke among Louis's courtiers (and a sitting joke if they'd been drinking) that, whenever the king wanted something accomplished, he would say, "Let Georges do it." This phrase has been singularly popular ever since.

O Henry!—Another eponymous gofer was Henry, a young American who toiled in George Williamson's candy company during the early 1920s. Sugar daddy Williamson had already named a chocolate bar "Baby Ruth" (after either his own granddaughter or President Grover Cleveland's daughter; the National Institute of Silly Candy Names is still investigating).

Nor was Williamson ruthless when it came to choosing a name for his next new treat (a peanut bar). Because requests shouted to the factory factotum Henry often reached the executive suite ("Oh, Henry, would you tote more peanuts over here?" and, whispered from the back storeroom, simply "Oh, Henry!"), Williamson called his new product "Let Henry Do It."

Oscar—As for the origins of *Oscar*, I'd like to thank my agent Jim Cypher, my editor, my publisher . . . oops, sorry! The nominees for most accurate etymology are: 1) It stands for "Obsessed by Sequels, Cash and Residuals"; 2) It's named for the vehicle driven by the Wizard in *The Wizard of Oz;* 3) It refers to the founder of the now-defunct studio, Metro-Oscar-Mayer.

May I push the envelope, please? And the winner is . . . Margaret Herrick, who, while librarian of the Academy of Motion Picture Arts and Sciences during the 1930s, observed, within earshot of a newspaper reporter, that the Academy's statuette looked like her Uncle Oscar. That figurine, by the way, was sculpted by artist George Stanley—yet another classic example of letting George do it.

Thy Name Is Woman!

Do you know what a *Liddy light* is? Before I dole out the answer, let's examine some other words derived from names of women, real and imaginary.

Ceres, the ancient Roman goddess of agriculture and grain, still feels her Wheaties in the English word *cereal*. When Italian astronomer Giuseppe Piazzi was scanning the area between Jupiter and Mars with his telescope in 1801, a huge asteroid hit his eye like a big Piazzi pie. It turned out to be the biggest planetoid ever found in the asteroid belt, and Piazzi named it *Ceres* because Ceres had always been associated with his native Sicily, a grain-growing region.

During the 1850s, American feminist and magazine editor Amelia Jenks Bloomer promoted a stylish new look for the "modern" woman: a short skirt worn over baggy pantaloons. Soon, sales of *bloomers* were blooming.

Fifty years later, women were panting again, this time over a new novel by Gelett Burgess featuring a sweet young woman on the cover. In a paragraph next to the picture, Burgess extolled the woman's beauty and identified her as Belinda Blurb. Ever since then, a brief write-up on a book jacket has been called a *blurb*. Burgess also invented the words *goop* (a boor) and *spuzz* (stamina). Fortunately, only *blurb* showed any spuzz.

Let's prance through elision fields to find two eponyms formed by the contraction of female names: *tawdry* is a contraction of *St. Audrey*, a seventh-century princess whose name somehow became associated with cheap necklaces, and *maudlin* is a shortening of *Mary Magdalene*, who was known for her continual weeping.

With *Melba toast*, we toast the coloratura soprano Helen Mitchell, whose stage name, Nellie Melba, honored her hometown of Melbourne, Australia. When Melba fell ill in 1897, her chef, Georges Escoffier, served her sliced toast, which unlike the diva herself, was very thin. Escoffier called it *toast Melba*, and, when she recovered, he served her a high caloric dessert of peaches, ice cream and raspberry sauce he called *peach Melba*.

It's time to put the brakes on this section—which brings us back to *Liddy light*. When Elizabeth "Liddy" Dole was U.S. Secretary of Transportation during the 1980s, she helped enact safety laws requiring a brake light in the rear window of new cars. Tailgaters, seeing red, called it a *Liddy light*.

Law Givers

According to *Murphy's law*, this book will have a mistake in it. According to *Parkinson's law*, it will take you as long to read this book as the time you allot to reading it. According to *Gresham's law*, this high-quality book will be driven out of business by inferior books. Hey, wait a minute!

Murphy's law, perhaps the best known of these three axioms, is usually stated as, "If anything can go wrong, it will." And, yes, there was a Murphy—Edward A. Murphy, to be exact, who during the late 1940s was a development engineer at the Wright Field Aircraft Lab in Ohio. In 1949, after tracing the malfunction of a cockpit gauge to faulty wiring by a colleague, Murphy said of the culprit, "If there's one way to do it wrong, he'll find it." Passed from one engineer to another and modified along the way, this dyspeptic observation became the motto of pessimists everywhere.

The British historian C. Northcote Parkinson first proclaimed his now famous law in 1955 when he wrote, "Work expands so as to fill the time available for its completion." In other words, if I know I have four years to write this book, it will take me four years; if I know I have only four months, it will take me only four months.

Parkinson made this astute deduction after an exhaustive study (what's that about work expanding?) of the British civil service, a sprawling bureaucracy that, like most bureaucracies, devoted most of its energy to perpetuating itself instead of getting anything done. Parkinson's 1957 book *Parkinson's*

Law, which was bound, appropriately enough, in red tape, made him the Patron Saint of Cubicle-land.

Another Brit, sixteenth-century financier Sir Thomas Gresham, gave us Gresham's law: people will hoard money of intrinsic value (gold coins), allowing money of less value (paper currency) to flood the market. Since then, Gresham's law has come to mean that inferior goods or ideas will always drive out those of higher quality. Thus, Spam outsells filet mignon and the Beastie Boys outsell Beethoven—not to make any value judgments or anything.

The Elusive Mr. Parker

You're walking through a crowded parking lot toward your car. A driver waiting for a parking space asks if you're leaving. What do you call that person? A *Nosey Parker* of course!

For many years, people assumed this term for a snoop or busybody was an eponym. Some have traced *Nosey Parker* to Matthew Parker, the Archbishop of Canterbury under Elizabeth I, who poked his holy honker everywhere as he sniffed out conspiracies against the Anglican Church. Others have attributed the term to the British sailor Richard Parker, who, in 1797, led a mutiny among British sailors posted at the mouth of the Thames. This petulant Parker, who apparently went nose-to-nose with the Admiralty once too often, was finally hanged from the yardarm of the *H.M.S. Sandwich*, becoming the first known example of someone with a nose for noose.

But according to etymologist Hugh Rawson, neither of these explanations is on the nose. The big problem with both derivations, he explains, is that *Nosey Parker* didn't appear in print until 1907, long after Matthew sniffed and Richard was snuffed. "The silence over the centuries, like the dog that didn't bark in the night," Rawson writes, "argues in favor of another origin."

Rawson surmises that *Parker* is slang for *park keeper* or for someone who frequents a park, especially London's Hyde Park (which explains the capital *P*). Because the inquisitive sense of *nosy* developed in the 1880s, Rawson theorizes that

Nosey Parker may have described someone who loitered in Hyde Park to spy on amorous couples.

But, in a concession to Victorian sensibilities, we avert our eyes for a moment to consider a less salacious explanation. As Rawson points out, *Parker* may be a variant of the dialect word *pauker*, which comes in turn from *pauk*, to be inquisitive.

Remaining Nameless

If you think Julius Caesar gave birth to the term *cesarean section*, that Thomas Crapper's name gave us a certain four-letter word, or that St. Peter's dwindling support for Jesus inspired the term *peter out*, keep reading. In fact, all these derivations are bogus. (The claim, by the way, that *bogus* derives from a frontier swindler named Borghese, has also proved to be bogus.) *Cesarean section*, *crap*, *peter out* and *bogus* are "false eponyms," words that appear to be based on people's names but really aren't.

Most of us have been told, for instance, that the delivery of babies by abdominal incision is called a *cesarean section* because Julius Caesar was born in this way. But, in Caesar's day, a mother wasn't likely to survive this risky operation. The fact that Caesar's mom lived for many years after he was born makes it highly improbable that his birth was accomplished by knife. (His death, however, was another matter.)

Whence *cesarean*? It comes from the Latin term *lex caesarea* (law of incision), which required that a baby be delivered by abdominal incision when a pregnant mother died close to term. The *caesarea* in *lex caesarea* comes not from Julius Caesar's name, but from the Latin verb *caedere*, meaning to cut.

It's true enough that in 1882 Thomas Crapper patented the siphon-and-ball device that made the modern toilet possible. But the noun *crap*, with the meaning it has today, first appeared in a slang dictionary eight years before Crapper first flushed. (At least credit Crapper with jiggling this handle. His name and gadget helped popularize *crap* as a slang term.)

And, while it's true that St. Peter's devotion to Christ waned temporarily on the night he denied knowing Him three times, you can't pin *peter out* on Peter. In fact, the term *peter out* didn't appear until 1846, when American miners first used it to describe veins of ore that had been exhausted. It may be derived from the explosive saltpeter used in mining operations, or from the French *peter*, meaning to explode weakly, to come to nothing. So the St. Peter theory peters out.

Name Droppers

"I'll change that name with you," says one actor to another in Shakespeare's *Hamlet*. Little did they know what they'd started.

Switch John Wayne's name back to Marion Morrison, and his macho image would wane. The *nom de gloom* Boris Karloff scares us, but his real name, William Henry Pratt, would bore us. And, as Shirley Schrift, Shelley Winters would surely get short shrift.

Many Hollywood name changers retain some shred of their given names: Woody Allen (Allen Konigsberg), Tony Bennett (Anthony Benedetto), Tammy Wynette (Wynette Pugh), Jack Palance (Walter Palanuik), Karl Malden (Mlden Sekulovich), James Garner (James Baumgarner), and Judy Holliday (Judith Tuvim; *tuvim* means holiday in Hebrew).

Sometimes performers' original names provide a secret clue to their success. The intelligent comedian Albert Brooks was born *Albert Einstein*. The cat-like Joel Grey was originally *Joe Katz*. Kirk Douglas (Issur Danielovitch) was sure of himself. And if Cher is without peer, she is also without LaPiere, her last name.

Separated at birth?: Michael Keaton (born Michael Douglas) and Michael Douglas; John Wayne and Janet Leigh (Jeanette Morrison); Ethel Merman (Ethel Zimmerman) and Bob Dylan (Robert Zimmerman); Suzanne Somers (Suzanne Mahoney) and Sally Field (Sally Mahoney); Winona Ryder (Winona Horowitz) and Moe Howard (Moses Horowitz); Talia Shire (Talia Coppola) and Nicolas Cage (Nicolas Coppola).

Red Foxx's real name, John Sanford, showed up in his hit TV series *Sanford and Son*, while Diane Keaton, originally Diane Hall, played Annie Hall in the movie of that name. In the 1940 film *His Girl Friday*, Cary Grant, born Archibald Leach, delivered this line: "The last person to say that to me was Archie Leach, just before I cut his throat."

Where do these aliases come from? Tuesday Weld (Susan Ker Weld) says *Tuesday* is a true Sue-donym: it's based on "tu-tu," baby talk for her real first name. During a stint as a bellboy at a hotel, Aaron Chwatt buttoned down a 48-button jacket—and his stage name as well: Red Buttons.

Engelbert Humperdinck, né Gerry Dorsey, took the gingerbready name of the German composer best known for writing the children's opera *Hansel and Gretel*. In fact, the original Humperdinck's brothers were so grim about this name-jacking that the singer uses only his first name when performing in Germany.

SHOP TALK

Words from Work and War

7

Whenever we're working, we're also wording. Whether it's the arcane jargon of a specialized craft, humorous nicknames for despised bosses or the subversive slang of employee discontent, we're inventing words and using them creatively. Many common English words began their working lives in the fields, factories, workshops and offices of civilian life, while others emerged from the barracks, barricades and battleships of military service. Whether we're *rookies* or *journeymen*, *strikers* or *scabs*, *privates* or *generals*, there's a term for our term of service.

Barnyard Epithets

No enterprise has planted more words in English than farming. Here's a bushel of agricultural terms:

harrowing—A harrow is a heavy wooden rake with many teeth used to smooth a plowed field for planting. If such a contraption were ever hauled over you, you'd probably understand why the word *harrow* is used to describe any frightening or distressing experience.

make hay—We all know that we should "make hay while the sun shines," but many people don't realize that "to make" hay doesn't mean to grow it, but rather to let it dry after cutting. That's why the sun has to be shining to "make hay." As Robert Frost wrote in his poem "Mowing," "My long scythe whispered and left the hay to make."

haymaker—When farmer Frost wielded his scythe vigorously, he was demonstrating the origin of the word *haymaker*, a powerful punch that resembles the motion of a scythe. *Haymaker* has come to mean any decisive stroke, such as a convincing legal argument or business tactic.

go to seed—If some leafy crops, like lettuce, are not harvested on time, they'll start to form seeds, making them inedible. So anything that deteriorates from neglect is said to *go to seed* or look *seedy*.

aftermath—In Old English, a *math* was a cutting of hay or grain, and *aftermath* was the grass that grew in a field after it had been cut. Today we still refer to the consequences of an event (usually negative) as its *aftermath*, as in "the aftermath of a hurricane." When students arrive in my history class just after taking a difficult algebra test, I always have to put up with the aftermath.

buy the farm—There are three possible explanations for this expression meaning "to die." Some say it originated among American soldiers during World War I when insurance policies were made available to soldiers in the then princely sum of approximately $5,000—enough for their survivors to buy the farm if they died. Hence, when a soldier died, he was said to have *bought the farm*.

A second explanation comes traces the term to RAF pilots during World War II who often shared pipe dreams about buying farms after the war. When a pilot was killed in action, his comrades would shake their heads and say he had "bought the farm."

But no crash course on *buy the farm* would be complete without this derivation: If a U.S. Air Force pilot crashes on a farm, the wreckage usually burns, thereby destroying crops, and polluting the land with hydraulic fluid, gasoline and lubricating oil. This keeps the farmer from planting there for several years. The farmer, of course, claims damages to his property from the Air Force. Since the farmer usually has a mortgage on the farm, the Air Force payment for damages allows the farmer to pay off his mortgage and he now owns the land free and clear, so the pilot has *bought the farm*.

Called by Your Calling

What do these last names have in common? *Faber, Goff, Manx, Ferrier, Kovacs, Herrero, Schmidt, Ferraro* and *LeFebre*. They're all international variations of the English name *Smith*. Somewhere among the ancestors of people born with these last names stands a brawny-armed, bellow-lunged shaper of iron—or maybe just a skinny little guy who enjoyed metalworking. In the spreading family tree a village smithy stands. That's why any couple checking into a motel as "Mr. and Mrs. Smith" is guilty of forgery in more ways than one.

The frequency of *Smith* and all its international Smithereens reflects the fact that every village needed someone to fashion and repair metal objects. (In future centuries, the most common last name will be *Computertechnician*.) Let's look at the job-related surnames I call *occunyms*.

Some are easy to figure out: *Carpenter, Baker, Shepard, Weaver* and *Guywhofixesblunderbusses*. Others are variants of familiar jobs: *Clark*/clerk, *Brewster*/brewer, *Faulkner*/falconer, *Baxter*/baker, *Chandler*/candle maker, *Bateman*/boatman, *Scully*/scholar, *Bailey*/bailiff.

But some occunyms aren't as obvious because they're based on archaic or little-used words. A *Crocker*, for instance, was a potter, as in *crockery*; a *Wainwright* was a wagon maker (*wain* is an old word for *wagon*); and a *Hayward* made fences to protect (ward) the hay.

A *Fuller* was someone who *fulled* woolen cloth by shrinking and thickening it. A *Fletcher* made arrows (the feathers on an arrow are still called *fletching*). A *Cooper* or *Hooper* was a barrel maker, a *Porter* a doorkeeper and a *Keeler* a bargeman.

The Twain twins Tom Sawyer and Becky Thatcher descended from a woodcutter and a roofer, respectively, while a forebear of Jimmy Stewart tended pigs (*steward* comes from *sty warden*), not six-foot tall rabbits. The last name of word weaver Noah Webster means weaver, while an ancestor of writer Ring Lardner was a keeper of the cupboard (larder). A forefather of folk singer Mary Travers was a toll-bridge collector (from *traverse*). And when one traveler couldn't pay up, he reportedly sang, "Michael, row your boat ashore."

Worders of the World Unite!

Look for the union label in this workaday glossary of labor terms:

strike—The term *strike* was first used to describe a work stoppage in 1768 when a group of angry British sailors demonstrated their refusal to work by striking (taking down) their sails.

Strike was used again just a few months later to describe a walkout by a group of disgruntled hat-makers (mad hatters), proving that the term had spread to other industries at the drop of a hat. As a labor term, *strike* first struck American English in 1799 when it was used to describe a ten-week walkout by New York shoemakers.

fire—This word, which became America's hot term for dismissal during the 1880s, comes not from blazing flames but blazing guns. It's a shortening of *fire out*, which in post-Civil War America meant to throw a person out. No other labor term has ignited more synonyms: *sack, boot, can, bounce, axe*. In today's euphemistic world, fired people are *outplaced, surplused*, and *riffed* (from *reduction in force*).

scab—Given the unappealing appearance of the crust that forms over a healing wound, it's not surprising that *scab* has been used in English since the sixteenth century to describe despicable people. In 1806, it went into labor, so to speak, giving birth to a new meaning: a person who replaces a striking worker by agreeing to work for lower wages. Do you think the displaced workers who coined this term were drawing a subtle analogy between a skin scab temporarily covering a wound and a human scab temporarily covering a job? Me neither.

yellow dog contract—In the dog-eat-dog world of labor relations, employers sometimes forced workers to sign agreements promising not to join a union. Though this practice started during the 1870s, the term *yellow dog contract* for such a pact didn't appear until the 1920s.

Nothing against Old Yeller or anything, but in American slang *yellow dog* has meant a mongrel or cur since the 1830s. By the 1880s it had come to mean a contemptible person. So how much respect did workers have for bosses who imposed yellow dog contracts? Not mutt.

Everyday People

Let's hear it for mediocrity! While eliciting only a lukewarm response from most people, the ordinary has actually inspired several fascinating words and phrases:

journeyman—In medieval times, a *journeyman* (from the Old French *jornee* for "day") was a competent craftsman who was qualified to work for a day's wages. A journeyman was more skilled than an apprentice but not as skilled as a master craftsman, so we still call an average performer in professions ranging from writing to plumbing, a *journeyman*.

ham-and-egger—Some eggheads suggest that this term for a boxer, actor or baseball relief pitcher of so-so ability comes from middling middleweights who made just enough money from their bouts to buy breakfast. Others have cooked up the idea that it was inspired by the uninspired banality of ham and eggs as a meal. Usually, a ham-and-egger is reliable and, when brought in as a relief pitcher, will at least keep your team from going from the frying pan into the fire.

run-of-the-mill—When you buy the "run" of any mill, whether the products be shoes, lumber or rumors, you're buying items before they are sorted and graded in quality. Because the run of the mill includes seconds and defective products as well as first-quality goods, this phrase has enjoyed a lengthy run as a synonym for average.

no great shakes—The varied explanations for this phrase are, in fact, no great shakes. It may refer to a low roll or "shake" of the dice, to a weak handshake or even to the Arabic word *shakhs* (man), as in, "the Sheik was no great shakes." Perhaps the shakiest (and nuttiest) explanation is that it comes from the negligible harvest that results when you shake a barren walnut tree.

mediocre—The word *mediocre* is derived from the Latin *medius* and *ochre*, literally meaning, "middle of the rugged mountain." Thus, while the outstanding U.S. leaders Washington, Jefferson, Lincoln and Theodore Roosevelt are carved at the top of Mt. Rushmore, passable presidents like Van Buren, Pierce, Hayes and McKinley should be sculpted halfway up the slope.

Hobby Till You're Hoarse

Have you ever noticed that a hobbyist—a stamp collector, for instance—will often rock slowly back and forth when deeply engrossed in his or her favorite pursuit? That gentle sway of total absorption provides a clue to the origin of the word *hobby*.

Back in the 1300s and 1400s, a small horse was called a *hobby*, and soon *hobbyhorse* came to mean a child's toy consisting of a fake horse's head on a stick. Because children rode their hobbyhorses with such energy and excitement, adults who pursued enterprises with similar vigor were said to be "riding their hobby." (They were also said to be out of their minds.) Soon *hobby* came to mean an activity pursued for pleasure outside one's vocation.

The French word for hobbyhorse is *dada*, a children's word for horse derived from *da, diva* (*giddyap*). Like the English *hobbyhorse*, the French *dada* came to mean a fixed idea or obsession. So when a group of poets and painters founded a radical art movement during World War I, they titled their journal *Etre surf son dada* ("on one's hobbyhorse") to express the intensity of their theories. Soon their revolutionary approach to art and literature was being called *Dada*, and movement leaders who had seduced female artists were being called "Da-da."

Like hobbyists, enthusiasts have an almost religious devotion to their pursuits. That's appropriate, because *enthusiasm* derives from the Greek *enthousiasmos*, meaning inspired by God (*theos* in Greek). When *enthusiasm* first appeared in English during the early 1600s, it referred to possession by God and later to the delusion that one was inspired by God. About 200 years ago, *enthusiasm* took on its present secular sense—great excitement or interest in a subject or cause.

If that enthusiasm becomes too extreme, we call it *fanaticism*, another word with a religious origin. In Latin, *fanum* meant temple. So the adjective *fanatics* meant of or relating to the temple and, by extension, inspired by a deity. When *fanatic* first entered English during the 1500s, it referred to excessive religious zeal only, but since then its meaning has broadened to include someone with extreme or unreasonable passion for any cause or activity. And, yes, *fan* is believed to be a shortening of *fanatic*, though, alas, no language enthusiast, hobbyist or fanatic has yet been able to prove it. Giddyap!

Wars of Words

In medieval times, instead of pouring oil on troubled waters, defenders of remote, moated and even outmoded castles poured oil on troubling marauders. Sometimes, just for variety, those who reigned rained hot tar or pitch on vicious visiting Visigoths. To heat up these viscous substances, they used a loggerhead, an iron tool with a long handle and a bulbous end bearing an uncanny resemblance to our current Prince Charles.

But if the indefatigable attackers, perhaps emboldened by large quantities of beer, managed to scale the walls, the defenders would use the loggerheads as weapons to bash back these lager-heads. Thus, we still speak of two opponents engaged in an intense, closely fought dispute as being "at loggerheads."

To expedite military communication during the American Civil War, army engineers would often suspend makeshift telegraph wires from one tree to another. After a few days, these wires would sag to the ground, resembling trailing grapevines. The reports and rumors soldiers received via this "grapevine telegraph" were said to come "from the grapevine" and soon *grapevine* became a general term for gossip or rumor among troops dodging grapeshot.

At the notorious Confederate POW camp Andersonville in Georgia, Union prisoners were forbidden to cross a railing about twenty feet from the camp's stockade. Because anyone straying beyond this boundary was summarily executed, it soon became known as the "dead line." After the war, *dead line* came to mean an inviolable time limit and was condensed to one word, probably by a writer rushing to meet a deadline.

Another term with a military origin is *hell-for-leather*, meaning at breakneck speed. *Hell-for-leather* can be an adverb, as in "Joan was driving hell-for-leather to the post office," or an adjective, as in "After the meeting, the faculty headed for the parking lot at a hell-for-leather pace." This expression was apparently coined during the late nineteenth century by British army troops in India. It originally referred to the hellacious beating leather saddles took when troopers rode their horses at full speed (to say nothing of the beating the horses themselves took).

The phrase first appeared in print in Rudyard Kipling's *The Story of the Gadsbys.* Not to beat a dead horse, but *hell-for-leather* later came to refer to speedy trips by other means—foot, bike, car, train, rocket ship, etc.

What about the origin of *doughboy*, a nickname for U. S. infantrymen during World War I? Donning my baker's hat, I'll knead the commonly given, wonderfully charming and probably inaccurate etymology. It comes from, of all people, Elizabeth Custer, wife of the famous general. In her 1887 book *Tenting on the Plains*, Custer wrote that Civil War infantrymen acquired this moniker because the globular brass buttons on their uniforms resembled "doughboys," the small, round doughnuts served to sailors on shipboard.

Yet, in 1867, just two years after the Civil War, a writer in *Beadle's Monthly* (which apparently delved into issues like this) claimed the origin of the term was "one of the inscrutable mysteries of slang." Hmmm . . . So, while some valiant etymologists are making a last stand around Custer's explanation, we more sagacious scholars resist such Armstrong/strong-arm tactics and conclude the origin of *doughboy* is uncertain. Yes, it's a bitter Pillsbury to swallow.

Finally, a parting shot. This term for a final insult or comment is most likely a corruption of *Parthian shot*. The Parthians, who lived in the first century BC, were such skillful archers that, even while retreating, they could stop and fire one last deadly shot at the charging enemy while simultaneously delivering one last jeer: "Have a nice day!"

Private Parts

AtteNNNNNNNtion!

The order of the day is to learn the origins of words for army ranks!

Private comes from *privatus*, a Latin word that meant not only belonging to oneself but also set apart from the state, deprived of office, which a lowly private certainly is. *Corporal* is a variation of *caporal*, from the Italian *capo* (head, chief). Some say *corporal* was influenced by the Latin *corpus* (body), making a corporal, appropriately enough, half head (leader) and half body (follower). But others lance that theory. *Sergeant*, from the Old French *sergent* (common soldier), is ultimately bilked from the Latin *servus* (slave)—which makes the term *master sergeant* something of an oxymoron.

Lieutenant derives from the Old French *lieu* (place) and *tenant* (hold). That's why *lieutenant* also refers to an official who acts in the place of a superior, as in *lieutenant governor*. A lieutenant is so named because he or she could serve in lieu of a . . . *captain*. This word kangarooed into English from the Latin *capitaneus* (chief), derived in turn from the Latin *caput* (head). (A French derivative of *capitaneus—chevetain—*became *chieftain* in Modern English.)

Major descends virtually intact (and in tactics) from the Latin *maior* (chief), while *colonel* marches all the way back to the Latin *columna* (column). Many theories have been advanced to explain why we pronounce *colonel* the same way we do *kernel*, but here's a "colonel" of truth:

A derivative of the Latin *columna* was the Old Italian *colonello* (the commander of a column of soldiers). French adopted *colonello*, but in the process changed it to *coronnel*, which became *coronel* in English. Soon some pedant, trying to reflect the word's Italian origins, changed the spelling of *coronel* to *colonel*. But, while the spelling changed, the pronunciation didn't, and that's why we still pronounce *colonel* as *kernel*.

I hate to generalize, but generals are called *generals* (from the Latin *genera*, kinds or types) because they're in charge of all kinds of soldiers, from privates to colonels—and sometimes even other generals.

At ease.

Names for Neophytes

During the American Civil War, some army recruits literally didn't know their left from right. To teach these greenhorns how to march, drill sergeants would sometimes tie a tuft of hay to the left foot and a tuft of straw to the right, and then shout "hay foot, straw foot," instead of "left, right." Soon Civil War recruits were being called *strawfoots*.

Several other terms for newcomers have marched into English in equally fascinating ways. Because unripened fruits and new twigs are often green, young oxen with immature horns came to be called *greenhorns*, even though their horns weren't really green. By the late 1600s, *greenhorn* was being used to describe inexperienced humans. The American West tendered us *tenderfoot*, a term first applied to imported cattle because they were tender-footed and later to inexperienced miners (and minors). Newly arrived easterners, who weren't used to wearing boots, were called *raw heels*.

From the Latin root *nova* (new) come *novice* and the French term *nouveau riche* (new rich), while tyro, meaning a beginner, descends from *tiro*, the Latin word for a fresh recruit. *Rookie* is traditionally assumed to be a corruption of *recruit*, but this origin has never been documented. Its first appearance in print came in Rudyard Kipling's *h*-dropping *Barrack-Room Ballads* in 1892: "So 'ark an' 'eed you rookies, which is always grumblin' sore."

Three possible sources of rookie are cited by Paul Dickson in his *Dickson Baseball Dictionary*: 1) from *rookery*, military slang for the barracks of new soldiers; 2) a jump from chess where the rook is often the last piece to be used when the game opens; 3) a play on *rook*, meaning to cheat, based on the assumption that new soldiers are easily cheated.

Other baseball terms for rookies include *busher* (a player just up from the bush leagues), *green pea*, *jelly beaner*, *huckleberry* and *kindergartener*.

In nineteenth-century America, country folk who had recently arrived in cities were often called *jays*, presumably after the birds. Because these bumpkins often ignored the city's pedestrian rules, they were called *jaywalkers*, a term we still use for such miscreants.

G.I. Jive

Just as World War II barracks, latrines and hulls of fifty years ago were emblazoned with the ubiquitous graffito "Kilroy was here," our language today still bears the unmistakable imprint of World War II slang. Let's look at some enduring terms from the war President Franklin D. Roosevelt preferred to call "The War for Survival."

Our phrase *Mickey Mouse* for anything petty or cheap comes from the World War II's Navy Military Indoctrination Centers, where unruly recruits, picking up on the center's acronym (MIC), called its picky regulations *Mickey Mouse*.

While you might assume *gremlin* has haunted us since the Middle Ages, this word was actually coined by the British Royal Air Force to describe the mythical little people who foul up the workings of airplanes. The fact that some airmen were drinking a brand of beer called *Fremlin* when they spotted these wee people explains the term *gremlin*.

Gung ho for enthusiastic came from *gōnghé* ("work together"), the motto of the Chinese cooperatives. In the South Pacific, U.S. Lt. Col. Evans F. Carlson made it the battle cry of his Second Marine Raiders, who soon became known as the "Gung Ho Battalion."

When we describe a major movie as a *blockbuster*, we're using a World War II term for a powerful bomb—but not quite as powerful as you might think. In Britain, where this term originated, *block* means a group of buildings, not an entire city block.

We still use *D day* to describe a target date, but no one is sure what the "D" originally stood for. Some said it was simply an alliteration; the French said it meant disembarkation; General Dwight Eisenhower said it meant departed date. I like Ike's.

Likewise, though most people attribute *GI* to "government issue," others contend it comes from the *GI* on Army garbage cans (for "Galvanized Iron"). John Kalafus of Washington, Connecticut, who served with the Ninety-sixth Infantry Division in the Pacific, told me he recalls it was an abbreviation for "General Issue."

As for the original Kilroy, the best evidence suggests he was James J. Kilroy, an inspector at the Fore River Shipyard in Quincy, Massachusetts, who wrote "Kilroy was here" on ship components to show he had examined them. Soon imitations of his sign-off were popping up everywhere.

Blowback

The most delicious moment in any action film occurs when the villain is "hoist with his own petard"—as when, for instance, a bomb he intends for others ends up blowing *him* up. But what's a *petard*, and why is someone *hoist* with it?

During the late Middle Ages, a petard was an explosive device shaped like a bell and stuffed with gunpowder. An army besieging a fortress would choose one or two unlucky fellows, called *petardiers*, to tiptoe up to the fortress, hang or lean a petard on its gate, light the fuse and run like hell.

Unfortunately for the petardiers, this device often exploded prematurely or flew backward at them after it exploded. So it wasn't uncommon for these poor souls to be hoist (lifted up, blown up) with their own petards. (The worst case scenario for these hapless petardiers must have been a fuse that fizzled after they had fled: "You go back." "No, *you* go back.")

Petard was originally the French word for—I'll try to put this delicately—breaking wind. Presumably, this device was so named because its report resembled a loud you-know-what. But I can't help wondering whether the military petard was so called because of its unfortunate tendency to . . . well . . . backfire.

By the early 1600s, writers were using "hoist with his own petard" in a metaphoric sense, meaning to be undone by one's own devices. In William Shakespeare's play *Hamlet*, for instance, Rosencrantz and Guildenstern are carrying letters to England ordering Hamlet's death. But Hamlet secretly replaces the letters, so the hapless couriers end up delivering documents that command their own executions. Describing his scheme, Hamlet says, "'Tis the sport to have the enginer hoist with his own petar . . . I will delve one yard below their mines, and blow them at the moon."

. Shakespeare's *enginer* is now *engineer*, of course, while *petar* was a variant of *petard*. His verb *hoist* was the past participle of the now archaic verb *hoise*, which had roughly the same meaning as the modern verb *hoist*. Because *hoist* is a form of *hoise*, not *hoist*, the phrase is still correctly rendered as "hoist (not hoisted) with one's own petard." So, if you really love this phrase, but use *hoisted* instead of *hoist*, you run the risk of being hoist with your own pet term.

THAT'S ENTERTAIN-MEANT
Words of Theater, Film, and Music

Many English words have gone through several stages—literally. We use theater slang, for instance, every time we take a *cue* from someone, *typecast* a stranger, bask in the *limelight*, give someone *top billing*, say he *fills the bill*, or describe him as a *trouper* or *ham*. Let's *tread the boards* and put theater terms *in the spotlight*.

Stage Struck

The scene: backstage at an off-off Broadway theater:

Ham: Did you ever notice how few words and phrases from the theater world have been big *box office* with the general public? Very few stage terms have *brought down the house* or basked in the *limelight*. Take a *cue* from me, most people *typecast* theater words; theatrical terminology almost never gets *top billing* in street talk, not even a *stage whisper*.

Trouper: Well, it's true that most people, even *stage mothers*, don't say *go up* when they forget something, as actors do when they forget their lines. And only a few realize that curtains are brought *in* and *out* from the *flies* (space above the stage) because *up* and *down* refer to stage location. But most people do know what it means to *upstage* someone.

Ham: Yeah, but theater words still don't *fill the bill* for the average person. Such terms may be *troupers* behind the scenes, but when it comes to enjoying the *spotlight* for a long run, it's *curtains*.

83

Trouper: I'm not saying that every theater term descends into common parlance the way the ancient Greeks lowered a *deus ex machina* (god in a machine) into their plays. But some people do know that *trod the boards* comes from medieval times when actors performed on wooden boards set up at the back of their wagons.

Ham: Yeah, but do they know *barnstormer* comes from actors who *storm* in rural barns? That to *strike* a set is to dismantle it? That *turkey* refers to a theatrical flop, *citronella circuit* to summer stock, and *blocking* to positioning of actors?

Trouper: Or that *ham* comes from the fact that indigent actors often use ham fat instead of more expensive cold cream to remove greasepaint? Or that *winging it* refers to relying on whispered cues from the wings when you forget your lines?

Ham: Hey! Just because I'm your *understudy* waiting in the *wings*, don't think you can *sandbag* me. *Break a leg.*

Trouper: Everyone knows we use that expression because it's bad luck to say "good luck" before a performance. By speaking aloud of one of the worst things that can happen to an actor, we remove the curse of its happening.

Ham: Then why is it considered bad luck to say the name of that Scottish play by Shakespeare in a theater, *Macbe . . .*
  A falling sandbag suddenly sandbags Ham.

Words with Character

What do the terms *lothario, braggadocio, simon-pure, mascot* and *ignoramus* have in common? (And, no, this doesn't have anything to do with your spouse's relatives.) They're all words derived from literary or theatrical characters.

The *lothario* scenario: In Nicholas Rowe's 1703 play *The Fair Penitent*, Lothario is an amorous rake who seduces many women. (One of his conquests, the beautiful Calista, repents of her infidelity and becomes the fair penitent of the title.) Thanks to this play, *lothario* soon became a common term for any playboy. Herman Melville even used it in his novel

Moby-Dick to describe a frisky male whale who leaves pods of blubbering females in his wake.

Another scoundrel, Braggadochio, is a swaggering braggart in Edmund Spenser's allegorical romance *The Faerie Queene*. Revealed as a coward, Braggadochio is stripped of all his glories: his shield, his lady, his horse, his squire, his beard, his cell phone. You have to be pretty braggadocious to lower the reputation of braggarts, but Braggadochio does it. Today we still call any boastful person a *braggadocio*, though the term is sometimes mistaken for an ice cream flavor.

In *A Bold Strike for a Wife*, a comedic play written by the English dramatist Susannah Centlivre in 1718, the devious Colonel Feignwell impersonates a Quaker named Simon Pure to win the hand of Miss Lovely. (Given the characters' allegorical names, this play could have been easily understood by Simple Simon.) Eventually, Simon Pure reclaims his own identity as the "real Simon Pure," purées Feignwell, and inadvertently adds an eponymous phrase to our language.

In the 1880 French opera *La Mascotte* (Sorcerer's Charm), the title character, Bettina, is a peppy, Sandy Duncan cheerleader type who brings good luck to the city of Pisa, which, considering the tilt of its tower, needed it. English picked up the term from this popular opera, changing its spelling to *mascot* and its meaning to a college kid in some goofy animal costume.

Ignoramus, meaning, "we do not know" in Latin, is the title character in a 1615 Cambridge University farce by George Ruggle. A foolish magistrate for the town of Cambridge, Ignoramus not only knows nothing, he doesn't even know he knows nothing. Bad combination. For Ignoramus it brings beatings, rejection in love, a shrewish wife, possession by evil spirits and confinement to a monastery, which, considering his previous life, must have been something of a relief. But soon the benighted Ignoramus was be-knighted as the patron saint of the clueless, and the word *ignoramus* lives on (except among those who have never heard of it).

Saturday Night Jive

Commedia dell'arte, the comic theatrical genre devised by traveling acting troupes in sixteenth-century Italy, was the "Saturday Night Live" of its day. In frenetic, madcap performances, full of slapstick, horseplay and obscene language, actors improvised lines and plots from standard situations and stock characters, hence its name "comedy of the artists." The zesty irreverence of commedia dell'arte influenced comedy from Molière to the Marx Brothers and set the stage for several English words as well.

One of the stock characters of commedia dell'arte was a Venetian named Pantalone, a thin, doddering old man who always wore slippers and tight-fitting trousers. So, when a similar style of trousers became popular in England during the 1600s, they were quickly dubbed *pantaloons*. During the late 1700s, *pantaloons* came to mean a certain style of wide-legged trousers, but by the mid-1800s, the clipped version *pants* was being used to denote any kind of trousers.

Another stock character in commedia dell'arte whose breeches bred an English word was Arlecchino, a genial buffoon with a masked face, shaved head and wooden sword. But what people remembered most about Arlecchino were his multi-colored tights. That's why an Anglicization of *Arlecchino—harlequin—*still means a variegated pattern, a pastiche.

Zany is derived from the commedia dell'arte clown Zanni (short for *Giovanni*). Because Zanni was a rascal who delighted audiences with his disguises, acrobatics and antics, we still describe anything bizarre or ludicrous as *zany*.

Perhaps the most disreputable "commedian" dell'arte was Pulcinello, a cunning, violent knave who eventually evolved into the pugilistic puppet Punch in British Punch and Judy shows. In these knock-'em-down playlets, the devious, dastardly Punch always escaped punishment for his crimes.

How bad were his crimes? Bad. In the original plot, Punch killed his wife and child but escaped from prison and snatched his soul back from the Devil. Punch's satanic self-satisfaction at continually eluding justice gave us the expression "pleased as Punch."

Pan Handles

Why is a negative review of an artistic work called a *pan*? That depends on whom you ask. Some authorities attribute the phrase to nineteenth-century American prospectors who used metal pans to separate gold from sand and gravel. When no gold was found, miners would say their ore hadn't "panned out." (Actually, when no gold was found these miners also said a lot of other words, most of them not suitable for minors.) Anyway, soon theatrical and literary critics began writing that failed books and plays "hadn't panned out," so, eventually, a critic who gave an artistic work a negative review was said "to pan" it.

But other lexicographers trace the term to a tamping bar used to pat down concrete or soil. The top of the tamping bar, called a *pan*, is repeatedly pounded or *panned* by a sledgehammer. So critics who hammered plays and books with similar force were said to *pan* them. Others say *pan* derives from cooking, where food is panned, that is, cooked or dressed in a pan. And, if you've ever seen what bacon looks like after being panned, you can see the similarity between being fried by a critic.

While the true origin of the critics' *pan* may never pan out, the derivations of three other theatrical terms are plain:

central casting—When someone's image perfectly matches a stereotype, e.g., the bespectacled professor, the imperious aristocrat, we say that person could have come from *central casting*. In fact, there really was a Central Casting Corporation. Established in 1926, it provided Hollywood movie studios with a pool of extras classified by type, such as "hick," "girlfriend," "city slicker," "girl-next-door" and "tough guy."

steal someone's thunder—In 1709, the British playwright and critic John Dennis rattled a sheet of tin to simulate thunder for his play *Appius and Virginia,* a production that apparently generated more thunderclaps than handclaps. A few nights after his show closed, Dennis attended a production of *Macbeth* where the same method of making thunder was used. Enraged, Dennis thundered, "They steal my thunder!" and the phrase rumbles in English to this day.

green room—The origins of *green room*, the waiting room where performers and guests relax before going on stage, has been traced to seventeenth-century Elizabethan theaters where such rooms often had green shrubbery in them.

Tipping the Scales

Did you ever wonder where we got the names for the notes of the musical scale ("do," "re," "mi," etc.)? Well, you see, a *do* is a deer, a female deer, *re* a drop of golden sun . . .

Actually, this musical denotation can be traced to the eleventh century when the eminent musician Guido of Arezzo was teaching his choristers a hymn honoring St. John the Baptist. "Take it from the top!" Guido shouted to his singers, apparently heedless of this command's ominous implication for the song's headless subject.

As the chorus sang, Guido was struck by the slowly ascending pitch of each line's opening Latin syllable: "*Ut* queant laxis . . . *re*sonare fibris . . . *mi*ra gestorum . . . *fa*muli tuorum . . . *Sol*ve polluti . . . *la*bii reatum . . . Sancte Iohannes." (Unfortunately, he was also struck by the musicians, who feeling they were underpaid, abruptly walked out of the rehearsal.) But from these six syllables, Guido devised a six-note scale: *ut, re, mi, fa, so, la*. "So fa, so good," he thought. Later on, when a seventh note was added to the scale, it was named for the initials of the last line, "Sancte Iohananes" (*si*). (Remember, Latin has no "J.")

Over the centuries, the English-speaking countries replaced *ut* with the more singable *do*, and, when that *do* had risen, the English declared it *ti* time, and replaced *si* with *ti*. This gave us the modern musical scale: $100 per hour for studio work; $200 for live concerts, much higher than the two drachmas per hour Guido's singers were earning.

The versatile Guido also gave us another English term. In his written notations, he used the Greek letter *gamma* to designate the lowest note on the scale, and later this note was called *gamma ut*. Eventually *gamma ut* was shortened to *gamut*, which came to refer, not only to the scale's lowest note, but to the entire singing range.

By the mid-1600s, *gamut* was being used figuratively to mean the full range of anything, as in the song "Home, Home on the Gamut." And we still say that something that ranges far and wide "runs the full gamut." "Run the gamut," of course, is not to be confused with "run the gauntlet," which refers to pledge initiation rites at Gamma Gamma Gamma.

Name Brand Bands

Folk singer Bob Dylan did not name himself for poet Dylan Thomas. Members of Led Zeppelin spelled their group's first name "Lead" as "Led" because they were afraid Americans would pronounce it "leed." And Pips of Gladys Knight and The Pips was the nickname of Gladys' cousin James Woods, who managed the group.

Given the traveling schedules of most groups, it's logical that many names are roadies: *Men at Work* (from Australian highway signs); *Chicago* (originally "Chicago Transit Authority"); *Buffalo Springfield* (from a sign on a steamroller listing a company's two locations); *Grand Funk Railroad* (after Canada's Grand Trunk Railroad); *Bread* (the band once got stuck behind a Wonderbread truck); and *Martha and the Vandellas* (a combo of Detroit's Van Dyke Street and lead singer Martha Reeve's favorite singer, Della Reese).

All's feral in love and rock, so it's not surprising that critters inspired many group names: *The Beatles*, of course, was a rhythmic take-off on *beetles*, while *The Animals* came not from the band's wild appearance, but from Animal Hogg, a member of the band members' street gang. *The Byrds* was inspired by a Thanksgiving turkey, and *Counting Crows* by an old English divination rhyme that says life is as meaningless as counting crows. *The Jefferson Airplane* named themselves after a friend's little dog, Thomas Jefferson Airplane, and *Procul Harum* was the pedigree name of a Siamese cat.

Many names are eponymous: *Country Joe and Fish* is a communist sandwich combining Joseph Stalin with a little Mao ("revolutionaries move through the people like fish through the sea"); *Pearl Jam* (after the preserves made by a band member's great-grandmother Pearl); *Jethro Tull* (eighteenth-century inventor of the seed drill); *Herman's Hermits* (a mishearing of *Sherman*, the name of the bespectacled kid in the Sherman and Peabody cartoons on TV's "The Rocky and Bullwinkle Show"); *Lynyrd Skynyrd* (from Leonard Skinner, the band members' high school gym teacher); and *Pink Floyd* (a blend of the names of legendary bluesmen Pink Anderson and Floyd Council).

And as for the true source of *Bob Dylan*, the answer, my friend, is blowing in the kin: Robert Allen Zimmerman derived his stage name from *Dillion*, the name of his uncle.

Talkies Talk

Have you ever wondered why the coming attractions preceding feature films are called *trailers*? In the early days of film, they followed or trailed the feature. Or why "George Spelvin" and "Harry Selby" appear so often in film and theater credits? They're fictitious names designed to conceal a performer's identity.

Another fascinating film term is *MacGuffin*. As the following newspaper quotations show, there's considerable variation in the term's meaning. From the *New York Times*: "[the late Alec Guinness is] perennially on the scent of the MacGuffin, the bit of magic that lifts a piece out of the common ruck." From the *Hartford Courant*, quoting filmmaker Ken Burns: "The MacGuffin in my Mark Twain film is his Hartford house. It's the symbol of escaping his boyhood. It's the symbol of tragedies that beset his family. And it's ground zero for his creative energies."

So is a MacGuffin a dash of magic or an essential symbol? Strict MacGuffinists would say neither.

The term *MacGuffin*, first used by Alfred Hitchcock in a lecture at Columbia University in 1939, is an element in a film, novel or play that provides a pretext for the plot. It may be anything—secret papers, jewelry, money—that propels the story. The MacGuffin itself has little, if any, intrinsic meaning.

MacGuffins in Hitchcock's own films include the stolen $40,000 in *Psycho*, the scientific formula in *The 39 Steps* and the smuggled microfilm in *North by Northwest*. Other cinematic examples include the falcon statue in *The Maltese Falcon* and the mysterious briefcase in *Pulp Fiction*. (Some contend Rosebud in *Citizen Kane* is a MacGuffin, but others disagree, claiming its meaning, revealed at the end of the film, is essential to illuminating Kane's life.)

But why *MacGuffin*? Hitchcock said the term originated in a strange story told by his longtime Hollywood friend, writer Angus MacPhail: Two Scotsmen are riding on a train when one man asks the other about the contents of a package on the overhead luggage rack.

"It's a MacGuffin," says the first man, "a device for hunting tigers in Scotland."

"But there are no tigers in Scotland," replies the second man.

"Well then, it's not a MacGuffin," says the first.

(As for spelling, most authorities prefer *MacGuffin*, in deference to the *Mac* of *MacPhail*, but *McGuffin* is an acceptable and common alternative.)

So the *Times'* use of the term to mean an uplifting turn of magic and Burns' connotation of a central metaphor both seem to have, well, a Hitch.

PLAYS ON WORDS
The Language of Sports and Games

9

English is a jock of all trades. It freely absorbs words and terms from many fields, rinks, courts and rings, often applying them to entirely new realms. Moreover, sports jargon is "teaming" with colorful phrases, many with intriguing derivations.

One Liners

No sport has enriched American language more than baseball has. With its eccentric characters, subtle strategies and leisurely pace, the field of dreams furnishes rich soil for colorful expressions. In fact, many baseball idioms and metaphors have pitched their way into common American catchphrases: *strikeout*, *pinch hit*, *heavy hitter*, *bush league*, *southpaw*, and *out in left field*, not to mention the notorious act of "getting to first base" and beyond. There's enough dugout dialect to keep an infield chattering all summer.

Baseball vocabulary is distinguished from the violent lingo of other sports by its understatement, indirection and mock eloquence. An inside pitch that nearly beans the batter is *chin music*, while hitting a line drive that just misses the hurler's head is *combing the pitcher's hair*. Likewise, a spitball is a *cuspidor curve* or an *aqueous toss*, while stealing a base as *purloining a hassock*.

Baseball eponyms abound: a fastball is a *Linda Ronstadt*, the singer of "Blue Bayou" ("blew by you"); a rookie who performs well early in the season is an *April Cobb* (as in Ty);

and a player skilled at orating against an ump's call is a *Daniel Webster*.

The summer game's pastoral origins sprout in phrases such as *grazer*, *orchardman* and *gardener* for outfielders, *ducks on the pond* for base runners, *barn door* for an easy pitch, *rhubarb* for an altercation, and *can of corn* for an easily caught fly ball.

Speaking of food, baseball's linguistic home plate is piled high. There's *ice cream cone* (a ball caught at the very top of a glove's webbing), *cookie* (an easy pitch), *pickle* (catching a runner between bases) and *cup of coffee* (a player's brief trial with a big-league team). Reflecting their hotel habitation, players call a ball that comes right to them *room service* and a home run a *dial 8* (the number dialed for long distance on a hotel phone).

But most of all, baseballers love synonyms. A hard grounder is an *ant killer*, *worm burner*, *grasser*, *lawn mower*, *daisy cutter* or *shin skimmer*. A good fastball is a *pea*, *heater*, *whistler*, *pneumonia*, *cheese* or *smoke*. And the ball itself is a *bulb*, *pill*, *marble*, *egg*, *apple*, *potato*, *punkin*, *sphere* or *tomato*.

Enough chatter. Play bulb!

English Goes Downhill

No one can *schuss* the many terms associated with the sports of the Winter Olympics. Here's a glazed glossary to help you track the traction, or lack thereof. What have you got to luge?

Luge, which rhymes with *rouge*, is that weird sport where a person in a Sue Pine position (no relation to Al Pine) descends over sheer ice at 180 m.p.h. vibrating like a skewered squid. *Luge* is a French dialect version of the Medieval Latin *sludia*, meaning a sled.

What about *bobsled*? *Bob* has many meanings, but the one we want is "to move up and down." According to the *New Encyclopedia of Sports* (I get by with a little 'alp from my friends), the bobsled was so christened because its riders often lean back and then bob up in unison to increase speed. Enough sled.

Moguls, the mounds of snow formed when many skiers turn at the same spot, do resemble human moguls; they're intimidating and can set your teeth—and skis—on edge. But, no, they weren't named for big shots who attract grand salaams like magnates. Some say *mogul* comes from a corruption of the German word *hügel* (small hill), some say from the Old Norse word *mügi* (heap). Some say just ski around 'em.

Telemarking, the technique for making long, slow turns in cross-country skiing, has nothing to do with those pesky salespeople who always telephone during dinner. It's named for the Telemark region of southern Norway. Likewise, the term *stem christie*, the expert parallel turn in downhill skiing, stems not from attempts to limit the St. Moritz ski vacations of actress Julie Christie, but from *Christiana*, Oslo's former name.

You might think the name of figure skating's rotating *axel* jump revolves around a wheel's axle. In fact, it comes around from Norway's big-wheel skater Axel Paulsen, who first iced this move in 1892. And a figure skater's *camel* spin is so called because a novice skater trying this difficult spin for the first time resembles a humped dromedary. Go figure.

English in Full Swing

Let's tee up some golf terms. Let's putter around with some links lingo.

I just took a writer's version of a *mulligan*, a second try from the first tee. The story goes that David Mulligan always drove his golf partners to the St. Lambert Country Club in Montreal, Canada, over a very bumpy road. To thank Mulligan for driving and to compensate for any shakiness in his hands from steering, his buddies always allowed him to take a second drive off the first tee. (Actually it was his *third* drive, counting the one in the car.) So whenever a player dubs a first shot and gets a second chance, it's dubbed a *mulligan*.

It's par for the etymologically coarse to assume that a golf course is called a *links* because its fairways are linked together like sausages. Actually, the missing *link* is the Anglo-Saxon word *hlinc*, which means rising ground, such as the ridges where the first golf courses were built.

The word *bogey* is also linked to an Old English word: *bugge* (demon). A century ago, the Englishman Hugh Rotherham assigned each hole a score—the number of strokes it would take a good golfer to play it. A song called "The Bogey Man" was popular at the time, and golfers began calling Rotherham's demonic scores *bogeys*.

Meanwhile, Americans, who were now using longer hitting, rubber golf balls, found the old *bogeys* assigned to their holes too easy. So, with the classic one-downmanship of Yanks, they yanked down the standard number of strokes for most holes by one, called these *pars* (Latin for *equal*), and used the old *bogey* for one over par. One-under-par play became a *birdie*, (*bird* was slang for *first-rate*), and two-under-par play was an even bigger and better *bird*—an *eagle*.

Etymologies still left holding the bag are *caddie* (from *cadet*) and *handicap* (from the swapping game, *hand in cap*). In the bag are *brassie* for #2 wood (after the brass plate on its sole) and *mashie* (from the same word that gives us *mace*, as in club). But even nibbling nitpickers have been unable to divot out the origins of the name for the nine iron with properties biblic—*niblick*.

Let the Names Begin!

Here's a handy guide to the origins of some Olympic terms:

In track, the *steeplechase*, a 3000-meter race including twenty-eight hurdles and seven water jumps, should ring a bell with equestrians. It's named for the country practice of racing steeds over natural barriers like hedges and streams to a church steeple in the distance. A preliminary race in track is called a *heat* because it heats up runners for the finals. By contrast, field event competitors who hurl objects and sometimes themselves through the air are divided into preliminary groupings called, appropriately enough, *flights*.

But there's an important difference between a heat and a flight. While the best runners are spread out (*seeded*) among the various heats so they don't knock each other off in the preliminaries, flights are usually grouped by ability, with the best athletes all in the same flight, hence the term *top flight*. In field events, distances thrown or jumped, not finishing place in the flight, determine finalist status.

Track trivia: The ten-meter zone in which relay-race runners can accelerate before they receive the baton is called the *fly zone*. *Pen-tath-lon* and *de-cath-lon* have three syllables, not four ("pen-tath-a-lon," "de-cath-a-lon.") You *put* the shot, *sling* the discus, and *throw* the javelin and hammer. The *hammer*, which is actually a ball attached to a wire and handle, is so called because sledgehammers were originally used for this event.

The dive called a *gainer* (a backward somersault) comes from a similar move in gymnastics in which the athlete lands slightly forward of the take-off spot, thus gaining distance. Some experts believe the term *pike* for a dive performed with bent hips and straight knees comes from the resemblance of this body position to the snout of a pike; others say this explanation is fishy.

Stroke!: *Coxswain*, denoting the person in charge of a racing shell, is a combo of *cock* (a ship's boat) and *boatswain* (a petty naval officer). The *crew cut* is named for the short haircuts sported by members of the Harvard and Yale crews during the 1920s.

Odds and ends: The *crawl* was originally called the *splash stroke*. Since *skeet* is an old word for *shoot*, the term *skeet shooting* technically means shoot shooting. *Soccer* comes from the practice of dramatically abbreviating "association football" and pronouncing *soc* with a hard *c*. *Badminton* is named for the Duke of Beufort's country estate in England where the Duke also enjoyed a drink of the same name made of claret, sugar and soda water.

Words That Ring a Bell

"The Heavyweight Corporation, already on the ropes after taking it on the chin from its competitors, suffered another body blow today when its president Horace 'Sugar Ray' Megamerger threw in the towel."

If this blow-by-blow description of corporate infighting has a familiar ring, it's probably because business writers use boxing terms so often to punch up their prose. The jargon of fistiana permeates our everyday conversation, too: *saved by the bell, low blow, black-eye, in the clinch, beat to the punch, hitting below the belt, down and out, lightweight, in your corner*. But overuse has taken the fight out of other phrases, and their boxing origins may no longer ring a bell:

Weigh in—Before a boxing match begins, both competitors must *weigh in*, i.e., stand on a scale to have their weights taken and recorded. Though this term eventually went upscale, its sense of reporting for a battle and making oneself known is retained in its current meaning—to express an opinion or give advice. ("He weighed in on the subject.")

On the button—*Button* is boxing slang for the end of the chin, a prime target for punches, so an accurate punch that landed directly on the chin was said to be *on the button*.

Handlers—Now often used to describe a political candidate's strategists and advisors, *handlers* is a hand-me-down from boxing where it refers to the trainers and "cut men" who repair and coach a boxer between rounds.

"We wuz robbed!"—This complaint, often uttered after a bad call by a sports official, is stolen from Joe Jacobs, manager of the boxer Max Schmeling. Certain that Schmeling had been cheated of the heavyweight crown in a bout with Jack Sharkey on June 21, 1932, Jacobs shouted this ringing protest into a microphone. Three years later, after leaving his sickbed to see his team lose in the World Series, Jacobs coughed up another ungrammatical but memorable catch phrase: "I should of stood in bed."

"Somebody up there likes me"—Research divines that this proclamation of heavenly favor descends directly from the title of a 1956 film based on the life of World Middleweight Champion Rocky Graziano, who was played by Paul Newman. Some say Newman "coulda' been a contenduh" for an Oscar that year, but apparently somebody up there didn't like him.

the real McCoy—Lexicographers have proposed many origins for this term, but have yet to find the real McCoy. The most popular explanation involves an American boxer named "Kid McCoy" who held the welterweight crown from 1898 to 1900.

Many other boxers imitated McCoy's deliberate style. So, in 1899, when McCoy knocked out Joe Choynski in the twentieth round, sportswriter William Naughton knocked out the memorable headline, "Now you've seen the real McCoy!" Later on, especially during Prohibition, genuine, uncut whiskey was referred to as *the real McCoy,* and the phrase never lost its punch.

Calling Cards

Let's play poker. Each time I provide the origin of a term, you decide whether I'm being *aboveboard* (playing above the table, i.e., honestly) or whether I'm *bluffing.* Be wary; I'm putting on a *poker face* and *playing it close to the vest.*

stand pat—This term, meaning to resist change, originally referred to poker players who were satisfied with the hands they'd been dealt. Having no need to draw any more cards, such a player was said to *stand pat* (*pat* meaning firm).

in the hole—In nineteenth-century gambling houses, slots or holes were cut into the center of poker tables with boxes attached beneath. During the course of a game, money won by the house was deposited into this hole, so losing players were said to be *in the hole*.

four-flusher—This derogatory term for someone who makes empty claims originally referred to a poker player who pretended to have five cards of the same suit (a flush), but really had only four.

pass the buck—In poker games, a knife with a buck-horn handle was passed from player to player to keep track of whose turn it was to deal or ante. Thus, *pass the buck* came to mean to shift responsibility to someone else.

play both ends against the middle—This term for playing two opponents against each other once referred to seeking the low and high cards of a straight. For instance, if you had the middle cards of a straight, say 6, 7 and 8, you'd try to draw the end cards (5 and 9) to complete it, thus playing both ends against the middle.

bluff—Poker players who pretend to have better cards than they actually do are said to *bluff*. That's because the false, boastful front of such a player resembles the steep bank called a *bluff*.

So was I bluffing with any of these explanations? You've called my bluff! There's no connection between the verb *bluff* and a steep bank. The verb *bluff* most likely comes from the Dutch *bluffen* (to boast).

Passwords

You're watching a basketball game on any playground in the United States. The ball rolls out of bounds to your feet. I absolutely guarantee you the players will not shout, "Please toss us the ball," or "Give us the ball," or "Ball!" Invariably, they'll shout, "Li'l help!" Shouting "Li'l help!" in such situations, in fact, is officially required by Article VII of the U.S. Constitution, and it's the first skill taught at pee wee hoop clinics.

And when today's *cagers* (now there's an old basketball term!) make a bad pass, they say, "My bad!" a phrase that seems to have dribbled into all walks of life. Now everyone says it, from the guy who bumps into you on the street to the teenager who dents your car to the stockbroker who loses your fortune. "My bad!"

In other hoop lingo, a player who can jump has *springs* or *rise*, a good player has *got game*, and a rebounder *crashes the glass*. A player whose shot has been blocked or *packed* by a defender *has Spalding on his forehead* (from the brand name imprinted on the *rock*). Deft dribblers are so deceptive they *break the ankles* of stumbling defenders.

And if a player has no defense (*D*), you drop the *D* from his or her name, as in *Onald*, and *Ebbie*. Likewise, players who can't hit the jump shot (*J*), are called *Erry* and *Ennifer*.

Of course, American speech has long been full of such hoopla. In business, a lame proposal is an *airball* or a *brick*, while a successful idea hits *nothing but net*. A skilled executive knows how to *box out* the opposition, put on a *full-court press*, *go to the hoop*, play *above the rim*, and *put the ball in the hole*.

When that executive triumphs, she shouts, *In your face!* to the competition. *In your face* originated in playground basketball, too; it's what you say to a closely guarding defender when you've sunk a shot—provided that defender is smaller than you are. If not, you may need more than a "li'l help."

Tennis Terms, Anyone?

The origins of many courtly words are as debatable as a line judge's call. *Tennis* itself entered Middle English about 1400 as *tenetz*, a word that showed up, racquet in hand, looking for a pickup game on a London court. Back then, *tenetz* referred to what we now call *court tennis*, a game played on a large indoor court with high walls.

It was on such courts in Paris that the National Assembly met during the French Revolution and issued the famous Tennis Court Oaths, vowing not to disperse before France acquired either a Constitution or pay-per-view cable coverage of the French Open. Today, of course, our tennis court oaths usually contain four-letter words.

Speaking of France, the Middle English *tenetz* may have come from the imperative form of the Old French verb *tenez*, meaning receive. Presumably, the player serving the ball would command his opponent, "Tenez!" ("Receive!"), and eventually the sport itself became known as *tenez*. (If named by this same method today, tennis would be called "Ya' ready"?)

As for the derivation of the courtly term *love*, tennis scholars have, appropriately enough, gone back and forth. Some suggest *love* comes from the Icelandic *lyf*, meaning something small or worthless, presumably what a tennis ball would be in Iceland. (I'll receive, no doubt, a chilly letter from the Icelandic Tennis Association, insisting the sport flourishes there on geyser-heated courts.) Others say *love* derives from *l'oeuf*, the French word for egg, reasoning that *goose egg* means zero in American English.

Nothing doing, says linguist Hugh Rawson. He suggests *love* may simply be a spin-off of the seventeenth-century expression, "to play for love," meaning without any monetary stakes, as in our expression "labor of love," a phrase I'd use to describe my own tennis game.

And why, you ask, is a serve that tips the net but lands fair in the service box called a *let ball*? Once again, the Word Guy is at your service! Because an archaic meaning of *let* is to hinder, impede. So a *let* ball is one that's impeded by the net.

Words of a Feather

What do your Toyota Tercel, your condominium at Wellington Mews and your expensive new fishing lures have in common? You haven't paid them off yet. (No wonder you look so haggard!) In fact, the words *tercel*, *mews*, *lure* and even *haggard* all swooped into English from the sport of falconry.

When the Normans conquered England in 1066, they brought with them not only a bunch of guys named Norman, but also their own style of falconry and fancy French words to describe its accoutrements. (How's that for a fancy French word?)

The Old French word *falcon* originally referred only to female hawks, while the male raptor was called a *tiercel* (*tercel* in English), derived from the Latin *tertius* (third). The fact that male falcons are about one-third smaller than females may account for *tercel*. A wild bird trapped for falconry as an adult was called a *haggard*, from the Middle French *hagard*. These haggards were often uncontrollable and difficult to train, and soon *haggard* was being used to describe unruly, intractable people, and, eventually, the gaunt appearance of an exhausted person.

Falconers summon birds back to their gloves by yelling esoteric commands such as, "Come back here!" and swinging a padded weight at the end of a cord. This device, called a *lure* (from the French *loire*), is often covered with feathers to resemble a pigeon, the falcon's preferred prey. Soon *lure* became a general term for any enticement.

When falcons become testy and finicky during their summer molting period, they are often confined to a cage or structure called a *mew*, from the French *mue* (molt), originally from the Latin *mutare* (to change). But, in later centuries, the falcons could not hear the falconers; things fell apart, and the center of these structures could not hold. So these mews were converted to stables, which, in turn, were often turned into houses or residential apartments.

The quaint word mews was picked up by upscale real-estate developers, and, to this day, you can still find an aspiring poet in a gated community, beseeching, "Inspire me, oh, Mews!"

Child's Play

Let's look at two intriguing phrases from children's games:

O'Leary—Although they don't realize it, kids who bounce balls through their legs and chant "One, two, three O'Leary" have a leg up on linguistic history. Folklorists Mary and Herbert Knapp have traced *O'Leary* to the Middle English phrase *a-lery*, an archaic term meaning lame or bent. A 1370 manuscript of the allegorical poem "Piers Plowman," reads, "Somme liede here leggis a-lery," meaning "Some made their legs crooked."

Ring around the rosy—For several decades, this children's rhyme has been plagued with the infectious rumor that it's derived from the British plague of 1665. According to this theory: 1) the "rosy" was a plague victim whose skin displayed the red rash of the disease; 2) people carried a carried a "pocketful of posies" because these herbs masked the stench of death; and "we all fall down" referred to the plague's high fatality rate.

But etymologist Hugh Rawson inoculates us against this contagious conjecture. If this rhyme, he asks in his book *Devious Derivations*, emerged from the plague of 1665, why does it not appear in popular songbooks until 1881? And why do the leading authorities on children's rhymes—Iona and Peter Opie—deride plague theory advocates as "would-be origin finders"? Ashes, ashes. The plague theory falls down.

Clothes make the man and woman. And they also make the meaning. From hats to boots, our language is attired (quite fashionably, I might add) in words derived from clothing, fabrics and other rai"meants."

Verbal Capers

Did you know the origin of the word *escape* is cloaked in a cloak? When you're trying to run away from someone, heavy apparel can be a peril. So you ditch that clunky cloak for a faster flight. The Romans referred to such close calls as *excappare*, literally, out of the cloak or cape. Eventually, *excappare* escaped into English through French, and soon any getaway became known as an *escape*, whether or not a cape was ditched in the process.

The cape also gives us the words *chaplain* and *chapel*. It all started when St. Martin of Tours, a fourth-century Roman soldier, ripped his military cloak in half and gave part of it to a shivering beggar (thus giving new meaning to the phrase, "how the other half lives"). Proud of his self-sacrifice, St. Martin wore the remaining half of the cloak over his shoulders as a cape for the rest of his life. When he died in 397, Frankish kings cherished this cape (*cappella* in Medieval Latin) as a religious relic.

These kings even brought this treasured *cappella* with them to war, but it was constantly getting lost in the fury of battle, producing dialogues like this:

Soldier #1: "Hey, Pierre, where'd you put that darn cape?"

Soldier #2: "I don't know where I . . . Look out behind you!"

Eventually, the French soldiers wised up and designated someone whose sole job it was to care for this *cappella* during combat. The chap they chose was reportedly so delighted when he first saw the cape that he sang out, "Ah, cappella!" (Appropriately enough, no army band was playing at the time.) This military custodian of the *cappella* was called a *cappellanus*, a word that eventually became *chapelain* in French, *chaplain* in English, and *Father Mulcahy* in American.

When the fighting was over, the kings toted the war-torn *cappella* back to the palace. There they placed it in a small prayer chamber. This room for worship soon took on the name *cappella*, which eventually became *chapele* in French and *chapel* in English.

Another word derived from the Latin word for cape is *chaperon*, which originally meant a hood or protective cape for the head. How *chaperon* came to mean someone who protects a young woman on a date, you can see easily (though you hope your chaperon doesn't see easily).

And speaking of hoods, During the 1500s, when the monk look was in style, and everyone wore hooded garments, thieves would often pull their victims' hoods down over the eyes during a robbery. Back then, *wink* meant to have one's eyes closed, so this practice was called *hoodwinking* or, if performed by the Prince of Thieves, *Robin Hood-winking*.

Bikinis, from Top to Bottom

How did Bikini, the Marshall Islands atoll where atomic bombs were tested in the 1940s and 1950s, give its name to the sub-atomic-particle-sized bathing suit introduced in France at the same time? Did a woman wearing a bikini affect men like an A-bomb? Did she seem as bare as a bombed atoll? Did bikini sales mushroom? Trying to cover this subject from top to bottom, I discovered, appropriately enough, a two-pieced etymology.

The first comes from Al Hefflon of West Suffield, Connecticut, who attributed *bikini* to naked avarice. "French fashion designers," Mr. Hefflon wrote, "had been planning a lot of publicity upon introducing their new bathing suit. Just before their news announcement, an atomic bomb test on Bikini Atoll captured the world's attention. The upstaged fashioneers said, in effect, 'We'll have our own bikini,' and they did their best to cash in on the news." Apparently, aggressive marketing was their strong suit, and bikini sales mushroomed.

(As long as we're in the bare midriff between the above explanation and the one below, let's belly up to the question of *monokini*. This term for a one-piece, topless suit is based on the mistaken assumption that the *bi* in *bikini* is the Latin prefix *bi-*, meaning two.)

Speaking of navel matters, our second etymology dates from World War II. U.S. forces in the South Pacific, explains Carl Williams of Lakeville, Connecticut, soon discovered that most atolls looked alike. (In fact, geologists tell us, nearly all atolls are dead ringers—circular coral reefs formed at the tops of dormant, underwater volcanoes.) Anyway, soon soldiers began referring to each atoll they encountered as "Nothing Atoll." (I'm not making this up.)

"Then, shortly after World War II and the A-bomb blast at Bikini," Mr. Williams writes, "*Life* magazine ran a picture of a Hollywood star perched in the back of a speed boat. She was wearing a *very* skimpy two-piece bathing suit (using the standards of the times), and my recollection is that the caption under the photo suggested that the bathing suit should be called a *Bikini* because it really was almost 'Nothing Atoll.'"

I guess that just about covers it.

Naked Truth

When we take off every stitch of clothing, we're doing *the full Monty*, a term popularized by the 1997 movie of the same name. Etymological detective Michael Quinion, who sleuthed the derivation of *the full Monty* on his Web page "World Wide Words," says this phrase has been British slang for "the whole thing" or "all the way" since the early 1980s. It first appeared in print about 1986.

Theories about the derivation of *the full Monty* abound. But, as Quinion reports, efforts to bare its true origin have, appropriately enough, proved bootless. Some postulations:

➤ It was invented by the British comedian Ben Elton as a substitute for *the whole shebang*.

➤ It's simply a variation of "the full amount."

➤ It derives from bales of wool imported from Montevideo. (Is someone trying to fleece us?)

➤ It comes from horse-racing, where *monte* has long meant a sure thing.

➤ It refers to being fully duded out in formal clothes rented from a British haberdashery called "Montague Burton."

➤ It denotes the large stack of cards on the table when the American card game monte is played. (In monte, by the way, the cards have *five* suits: clubs, diamonds, hearts, spades and birthday.)

➤ It's somehow (don't ask!) derived from *Monty Python's Flying Circus*.

➤ It's linked to a colorful bloke named Lord Montague of Beaulue.

➤ It's an eponym that refers to the impressive appearance of British Field Marshal Bernard Law Montgomery (known as "Monty") whenever he wore his full complement of medals.

The most persuasive explanation also involves Field Marshal Montgomery, but in a different way. Montgomery, no matter where he was or what battle was raging, always insisted on being served a full English breakfast (eggs, bacon, beans, a broiled tomato or mushroom, toast, marmalade and tea). If you order *the full Monty* at a working-class café in the north of England, you will be served the same huge breakfast Monty devoured. Thus, the phrase has come to mean "to go whole hog."

As someone who soldiered through several full English breakfasts during my honeymoon in Britain ("No, I *don't* want your broiled tomato, honey!"), I'm swallowing this Baconian reasoning. In fact, I will forever capitalize the *M* in *the full Monty* to reflect its eponymous origin.

Spin Control

According to a recent newspaper report, a new sci-fi flick features a "little toe-headed lad." True, such a grotesque creature might appear in a futuristic film. But I'll bet the writer meant *tow-headed*, one of many terms derived from the old-fashioned enterprise of spinning.

Coarse flax or hemp prepared for spinning is called *tow*. Because tow is yellowish in color, people with blond hair came to be called *towheads*. Soon they formed a support group with the motto, "Towheads are better than one." (My favorite towhead in literature is Sir Andrew Aguecheek, the numbskull nobleman in William Shakespeare's *Twelfth Night*, whose yellow mane is wonderfully described as hanging "like flax on a distaff.")

A *distaff* is the short staff or stick that holds the tow. Because the task of spinning fell largely to women, the distaff became an emblem of women's work. Eventually, *distaff* came to refer to the realm of women and to women collectively. Speaking of Twelfth Night, the day after the twelve days of Christmas was called *Distaff's Day* because that's when women ceased their holiday baking and hosting and returned to their spinning. Until the 1980s, it was common to hear people say *distaff side* to refer to women, especially to women's sports. But the gender bias of this term has rendered it as archaic as a spinning wheel. Good riddance!

Another sexist term associated with spinning—*spinster*—is also, mercifully, dying out. *Spinster* originally referred to any person who spun, regardless of that person's gender. But during the 1700s it became a disparaging term for an older woman who had never married.

And, if you feel like heckling the inventor of Distaff's Day, you should know that *heckle* also comes from spinning. Before flax is spun, its individual stems are separated and combed in a process called *heckling*. This notion of picking something apart and finding its defects gave us the term *heckle*. I can't help picturing wiseacre flax combers yelling, "Hey, flax, you stink!" and "Ya call that funny?!" Talk about needing new material!

Hat Tricks

Hold on to your hats as we explore the heroes and heroines beneath the headgear.

The fedora, beloved by gray-flanneled commuters of the 1950s, was inspired by the soft felt hat worn by Fédora, the (female) title character of an 1882 play by French writer Victorien Sardou. You have to take your hat off to the fedora, a style popularized during the 1880s that remained fashionable until John F. Kennedy took his hat off in the 1960s (though apparently somebody forgot to tell Karl Malden, who never left home without it).

The derby is named, in a roundabout way, for Edward Stanley, the twelfth earl of Derby. It all began in 1780 when he founded a horse race at Epsom Downs, England, that became known as "the Derby." This race, in turn (actually, a clubhouse turn), inspired the name "Kentucky Derby." So when hat makers of the 1880s introduced a new style of felt hat with a round crown and a curved brim to American males, they marketed it as "the overwhelming favorite of men at the Kentucky Derby," and this hat became known in the U.S. as the "mint julep."

(Have you ever wondered why people wore "felt" hats, and not "handled" or "groped" hats? Me neither.)

Meanwhile, back in England, *derbies* were known as *bowlers*, and, no, it wasn't because they were shaped like bowls. The London haberdasher who first sold these domes in the 1860s was named "Bowler." One ad for Bowler's new hat read, "The head is relieved of the pressure experienced in wearing hats of the ordinary description." A century later, James Bond's cinematic nemesis Odd Job would use a steel-rimmed bowler to relieve people of the pressure experienced in having a head.

Let's put this mad hattery to West. The Stetson worn by cowboys was the stepson of John Batterson Stetson. While visiting the western gold fields during the 1860s, Stetson noted the high-crowned, wide-brimmed hats worn by prospectors. He returned to the East, hat in hand, and soon his Philadelphia factory was producing two million Stetsons a year.

Hat's all, folks!

To Boot or Not to Boot

Ever wonder why *to boot* means besides? I'll tell you—and boot up some lore about the word *boot* to boot!

First, you need to know that there are two kinds of *boot* in English—and, as with the boots you wear, only one is left. The archaic meaning of *boot*, from the Old English *bot* (help), means remedy, deliverance, avail. It's this meaning that survives in the idiom *to boot*, meaning to the good, besides, moreover. This sense of *boot* also lingers in the rarely used verb *boot* (to help), and in the nouns *booty* (plunder) and *boot*, a Southern U.S. term for a small item thrown in to equalize a trade.

This meaning of *boot* also surfaces in Shakespeare's *Julius Caesar*. A moment before Caesar is assassinated, he declares he will not be swayed, even by the genuflection of his good friend Brutus. "Doth not Brutus bootless kneel?" he asks. Does this mean Brutus removed his boots as an act of supplication? Nope. Here *boot* means avail, advantage, so Brutus wasn't without boots; he was without boon.

The footwear type of *boot* stepped into English from the Middle French *bote*. As a verb, this *boot* can mean kick, throw out, inject a drug, flub something (such as a grounder in baseball), put boots on, or vomit (not necessarily in that order). As a noun, it can mean a summary dismissal ("get the boot"), momentary pleasure ("get a boot out of it"), or a Marine Corps recruit (from "boot camp").

Boot also boasts an impressive auto-biography: it denotes a trunk (in Britain), a covering for the base of a stick shift, and a device affixed by police to the wheels of scofflaws' cars (*Denver boot*). Its colorful compounds include *bootlicker, bootlegger,* and *bootstrap* (to accomplish something on one's own), from the expression "pull yourself up by your own bootstraps." *Bootstrap* gives us the computer term *boot,* meaning to start up a computer program. A *bootstrap loader* is a small program that, when moved into memory, will load the rest of the system and start (boot) it up.

So *boot* has gone from footwear to software. Isn't that a kick?

More Fabrications

all wool and a yard wide—During the 1800s, dishonest textile merchants tried to fleece customers by passing off inferior fabrics as 100 percent wool and by selling "yards" of cloth that were slightly less than thirty-six inches wide. Fortunately, honest wool dealers made a valiant stand on the one-yard line. Their fabrics, they assured sheepish customers, were "all wool and a yard wide."

shoddy—During the American Civil War, the uniforms of Union soldiers were often made of shoddy, an inferior woolen fabric that sometimes dissolved in a hard rain or fell apart after a day's march. Officers, already worried about soldiers deserting their outfits, now had to worry about outfits deserting their soldiers. It's no wonder that the adjective *shoddy* was soon being applied to any poorly made item.

the whole nine yards—Some say this term came from the realm of fabrics where a full-length bolt of cloth sometimes measures nine yards long.

But two other explanations have equal support among scholars. On old-style concrete trucks, a full load was nine cubic yards, so customers often ordered and received "the whole nine yards." Others say the term refers to the ammunition belts of World War II fighter planes, which were exactly nine yards long. So any pilot who used an entire belt was said to have given the enemy "the whole nine yards."

pants—This mundane word has a surprisingly spiritual origin. It began with a fourth-century Roman Catholic saint named Pantaleone. Because Pantaleone served as the patron saint of Venice, inhabitants of that city became known as "Pantaloni."

When Italy developed the form of theater *called commedia dell'arte* during the 1500s, one of its stock characters was "Pantalone," a wealthy but miserly Venetian merchant. Pantalone wore tight-fitting trousers, so, when similar trousers became popular during the late 1700s, they were called "pantaloons." Soon "pantaloons" came to refer to trousers in general. During the early 1800s, Americans shortened "pantaloons" (the word, not the garment) to "pants," and, until the early 1900s, many still considered "pants" a vulgarity. (In fact, I have some 1970s pants in my closet that many still consider a vulgarity.)

Jean Pool

Back in sixteenth-century England, a new type of twilled cotton fabric was all the rage. (Well, OK, so only seven snooty duchesses could afford it, but no matter.) Imported from the Italian city of Genoa, this durable material was called *jean fustian*. *Jean* was Middle English for *Genoa* and *fustaneum* was Medieval Latin for cotton or linen fabric. (Hmmm . . . Jean Fustian. I think I sat behind her in eleventh-grade English.)

Soon *jean fustian* was shortened to *jean,* and the trousers made from this fabric were being called *jeans*. So, oddly enough, the man who first discovered America (Columbus) and the fabric that eventually covered America (jeans) both came from Genoa.

As if that wasn't coincidence enough, another name for this same fabric—*denim*—derives from another city on the Mediterranean—Nimes. In this bustling textile center, the French manufactured a durable twilled fabric called *serge de Nimes* (serge of Nimes). *Serge* derives from the Latin *sericus*, meaning of silk.

During the seventeenth century, the term *serge de Nimes*, along with a bunch of the fabric itself, was brought to England, where it was rendered as *serge denim*. Eventually, this was shortened to *denim*, and the trousers made of denim were shortened to cut-offs.

Jeans and denim are two of many fabrics and garments that are ready-to-"where." Can you match the apparel with its place of origin or association?:

Locution: 1) jersey 2) poplin 3) calico 4) muslin 5) cashmere 6) worsted 7) argyle 8) cravat

Location: a) Avignon, France b) town in county of Norfolk, England c) Croatia d) county in Scotland e) mountainous region on the border of India and Pakistan f) wool-producing island in the English channel g) city in India h) city in Iraq

Answers:

1-f. The island of Jersey was famous for its knit garments.

2-a. Avignon was a papal town, a "papalina" in Latin.

3-g. Calico was first imported from Calicut, India.

4-h. Muslin comes from Mosul in Iraq.

5-e. Cashmere wool comes from goats in Kashmir in the western Himalayas.

6-b. This smooth, compact wool yarn originated in Worsted, England (now Worstead).

7-d. Its diamond pattern is an adaptation of the tartan of the Campbell clan from the Scottish county of Argyllshire.

8-c. Croatian mercenaries in the service of France wore these bands of fabric around their necks; the French word for a Croatian was *Cravate*.

Body English

When the Victoria's Secret specials air on TV, we prudent protectors of grammar, usage and western civilization are watching—with purely academic interest, of course. We judiciously avert our eyes during any inappropriate displays, such as dog food commercials.

Hold on a minute while I slip into something more comfortable . . .

You might wonder whether a negligee, a woman's long, flowing dressing gown, has something to do with neglect. I know I always have. In fact, *negligee* derives from the same root as *neglect*—the Latin *neglegere*, to neglect.

Originally, *negligee* referred to a long necklace of irregular beads or coral. It was so named because this random collection of trinkets seemed to be assembled out of carelessness or negligence. Eventually, *negligee* came to denote a similarly casual garment, often made of soft, delicate fiber.

Because *lingerie*, a fancy word for women's underwear, is sometimes worn while lounging, you might assume it's derived from *linger*. Sorry. *Lingerie* comes from the Latin word for linen, *lineus*—and that's no fabrication. In fact, an archaic meaning of *lingerie* is linen articles or garments.

It's appropriate that a groom gets down on bended knee to remove his bride's garter. For *garter* derives from the Celtic *garet*, meaning the bend in the knee, which is approximately the spot—avert your eyes here—where this band is worn to hold up a stocking or sock. A *garter snake* is so called, not because it slithers up legs in search of garters—eeeek!— but because the longitudinal stripe on its back resembles a band or garter.

If the lacy lingerie ensnares our eyes it may be because *lace* originally meant a snare or noose. This sense survives in *shoelaces*, which are tightened to secure footwear. Eventually, *lace* came to denote cords or threads that are interwoven.

Both *chemise* (a one-piece undergarment) and *camisole* (a short negligee jacket) derive from the Late Latin *camisia*, shirt. A chemise is also known as a *teddy*, a term that first appeared during the 1920s. Some have tried to connect this term to *teddy bear/bare* or even Teddy Roosevelt (whom you *never* want to picture in a teddy). But, about the true origins of *teddy*, we know, appropriately enough, next to nothing.

ONE-TERM WONDERS
Words of Government and Politics

Politicians have been responsible for some of the highlights (Lincoln's "of the people, by the people and for the people") and lowlights of language (Clinton's "That depends on what the definition of 'is' is"). The language of government and politics is certainly full of evasion, euphemism and ebullience, but it has also produced and popularized some of our most colorful and captivating expressions.

Vox Pop, You Lie

As a campaign gimmick during the 1840 presidential election, supporters of William Henry Harrison pushed a ten-foot leather ball from town to town. (Now *that's* spin control!) Written on the ball were the words "Keep the Ball Rolling," a slogan that still rolls along in our language. Let's examine some other political terms:

candidate—Picture your candidates for the local school board walking around in white togas. Now stop laughing. In ancient Rome, men running for office wore white togas rubbed with white chalk to suggest that their characters were spotless. Stop laughing again! Because the Latin word for white was *candidus*, they were called *candidati* (along with a lot of other names I can't repeat here). *Candidati* comes from the Latin *candere* (to shine), which still glows in *candid* and *candle*.

hustings—Just what are those hustings candidates are always going out on? The answer comes from Old Norse, where *husthing* meant assembly house. *Husthing* became *husting* in Middle English, denoting a court of common pleas.

Because such courts were sometimes used for political speeches, *hustings* also came to refer to the raised platform on which political candidates speak (hence, the expression "on the hustings"). Eventually *hustings* became a general term for the all the hoopla—baby kissing, handshaking, speechmaking—associated with an election campaign.

caucus—This term for a meeting of local party members to express preferences for candidates or delegates comes from an Algonquin word for a tribal counselor or leader. First recorded in English by Captain John Smith as *cawcawwassoughes*, it was later condensed to *coucorouse* and eventually *caucus*. As the length of this word shrank, its meaning expanded to mean a group of leaders or citizens with a common political interest.

ballot—Ever since ancient times, small balls, sometimes marked or colored, have been used for secret voting. In Renaissance Venice, such a ball was called a *ballota* (little ball). The British adopted this Italian term as *ballot*, and used it to refer any device for casting a vote.

filibuster—This term for a legislative tactic designed to obstruct passage of a bill by prolonging debate and delaying a vote originally had more to do with piracy than politics. *Filibuster* comes from the Dutch word *vrijbuiter*, meaning freebooter or sea raider. The Spanish later adopted *vrijbuiter* into their language as *filibustero*.

During the nineteenth century, Latin Americans used *filibustero* to describe the piratical Yankee adventurers who brazenly tried to set up pro-American governments in their lands. Perhaps the most famous American filibusterer was William Walker, who established his own short-lived regime in Nicaragua during the 1850s.

Soon *filibuster* entered American English as a term for any kind of freebooting operation, including the attempt to tie up a legislative body with interminable talk.

gerrymander—*Gerrymander* means to shape the boundaries of a legislative district so it includes a majority of voters favorable to a particular candidate or party. The term comes from U.S. politician Elbridge Gerry (1744-1814), who, as governor of Massachusetts, slyly redrew the state's U.S. congressional districts to favor his own Democratic-Republican party.

One of the new districts snaked so obviously and awkwardly across half the state that it looked like a huge salamander. Soon the compound word *gerrymander* was coined to describe this politically motivated monstrosity. (Interestingly, Elbridge pronounced his last name with a hard *g*, like the name *Gary*, but *gerrymander* is usually pronounced with a soft *g*, as in *Jerry*.)

hell-bent for election—This American expression apparently originated during the Maine gubernatorial campaign of 1840. Edward King, a Whig, was running for governor of Maine against the incumbent John Fairfield, a Democrat.

King, who had been unseated by Fairfield in the previous election, was so determined to win the rematch that he was said to be "hell-bent for election." In fact, King's victory song included these lines: "Oh, have you heard how old Maine went? She went hell-bent for Governor Kent." (OK, so it's not exactly Snoop Dogg.)

The *bent* in this phrase means strongly inclined, intent, as in "He was bent on going." So someone who is hell-bent on something will pursue a goal, even if it means going to hell. *Hell-bent for election* isn't limited to politics. It's used to describe any obsessive hankering, whether the goal is power, money or love.

stemwinder—A mainstay of nineteenth-century politics was the stemwinder—a bombastic, long-winded speech. In the days of stem-winding pocket watches, it referred to an oration that lasted so long you had to wind your watch to keep it from running down.

Interestingly, this political use of *stemwinder* contradicted an earlier meaning of the term. The first stemwinders were watches. Winding a watch required a winding key until the late 1800s, when watches were invented that were wound by a pin through the stem. These newfangled stemwinders were such a marvel that *stemwinder* came to refer to any person or thing considered first-rate.

So how did the original noun with the positive meaning of excellent, first-rate acquire a meaning of tedious, long-winded? Were the folks who devised the first meaning ignorant of the second meaning? Or did they, with a dash of irony, concoct the second meaning to subvert and mock the first? That could be subject of a long-winded oration.

pundit—A pundit is a commentator, usually on political events. While *pundit* might seem like a relatively recent term, it first appeared in the 1600s, an era when spin-doctors would often try to cure political campaigns with leeches. (Now the spin-doctors *are* leeches.) *Pundit* comes from the Hindi word *pandit*, meaning a learned man or teacher. Though some pundits do make puns, the origins of the words *pundit* and *pun* are unrelated. *Pun* may come from the Italian *puntiglio*, a fine point or quibble, but no one knows surely, not even Shirley.

Dead Lines

Politics, with its eleventh-hour negotiations and down-to-wire votes, uses a variety of words to describe desperate, last-minute enterprises:

endgame—In chess, the endgame is the final portion of the game when most of the pieces have been removed from the board. During the endgame, the king (President) becomes a very active and important piece, and even the lowliest pawn (first-term Congressperson) may suddenly become very valuable.

Perhaps because it's often been linked with nuclear confrontation, *endgame* has taken on a particularly ominous connotation. Playwright Samuel Beckett enhanced this fatalistic tone when he titled one of his existential plays *Endgame*.

last-ditch effort—In 1672, William, Prince of Orange, was asked whether he thought his country, England, would be defeated by France. "Nay, there is one certain means by which I can be sure never to see my country's ruin," he replied, leaving royal scribes scratching their heads. Fortunately, his next line was more intelligible: "I will die in the last ditch."

Realizing that clear syntax was not his forté, William stuck to forts, didn't die in the last ditch and eventually became King William III, an active and important chess piece during the endgame of the British Empire. And we still dig *last ditch* as a description for a final, desperate effort.

eleventh hour—Doesn't the phrase *eleventh hour* refer to the hour between 11 PM and midnight even though that's technically the twelfth hour? Nope. It comes from Jesus' parable (Matthew 10:1-16) about the boss who paid the same wage to workers who arrived at the eleventh hour of the work day (between 4 PM and 5 PM), as he did to those who had already put in a ten-hour day.

Bureau-crazy

When government gets big and complicated, the words to describe its projects and problems get crazier. It's hard to believe, for instance, that a massive *boondoggle*, such as Boston's Big Dig, with its enormous delays and cost overruns, could be named for a something as modest as a braided leather cord made by Boy Scouts, but it is. During the 1920s, American scoutmaster A. H. Link applied the term *boondoggle* to these trivial doohickeys used as neckerchief slides, hat bands or ornaments. And that's the link: a boondoggle, like the plaited cords, is a time-wasting, make-work project.

(Scholarly efforts to prove the word came from a frontier term for gadget, Daniel Boone's doggie toys, iron smelting or the Tagalog word *boondocks* have all ended in boondogglery.)

Boondoggles usually involve a lot of rigmarole and red tape. The origins of *rigmarole* began during the Middle Ages when people would write out a series of poetic verses on a roll of paper and attach a separate string to each verse. Each player would randomly choose a string and then read the verse affixed to it, which was interpreted as an amusing description of the person who chose it. Today we call this *Hollywood Squares*. The roll used in this game was called a *Ragman roll*, and soon any complex or ritualistic procedure came to be called *rigmarole*, whether or not any actual rolls were involved.

Later on, during the Victorian era in England, red tape was used to tie up large packets of government documents. As the British bureaucracy expanded, citizens who felt tied up by it started referring to its many entangling rules as *red tape*. Another bane of bureaucracy, deficit spending, is called *red ink*. This term originated with the practice of recording financial losses in red ink.

Swear Words

Priests are ordained, lodge members are inducted and plumbing is installed, but why do we say that a U.S. president is *inaugurated*? To find out, we have to auger through many layers of linguistic history, all the way back to ancient Rome.

The Romans believed the will of the gods could be divined by observing birds, and thus they assigned certain wise—and presumably far-sighted—men to note and interpret every feathery feat: the types of birds, their songs, numbers, times of appearance, direction of flight, even diet.

From such avid avian observations, these early birders made predictions about future events and determined whether the gods looked favorably on planned enterprises. In fact, no ceremony, large or little, was scheduled without first checking the birds, the same way we ultra-sophisticated, twenty-first-century types consult a horoscope.

At first, the Romans called a fowl-weather forecaster an *auspex*, a combination of the Latin *avis* (bird) and *specio* (to see). Any prophetic token or sign came to be known as an *auspicium*, the root of our English word *auspice*, meaning favorable sign. By extension, *auspice* means benevolent protection or support, as in "auspices of the United Nations." Likewise, an auspicious occasion or circumstance is favorable or successful.

Later in Roman times, a bird-based futurist was known as an *augur*, a combination of *avis* and *garrio* (chatter), and his chatty prediction was called an *augurium*. Thus the English word *augur* means to make predictions, and we say that a favorable sign "augurs well" for an upcoming enterprise.

(The word *auger*, by the way, meaning a tool for boring in wood or ice, doesn't come from Latin. Unless medieval wheel hubs especially fascinate you, its origins are, well, boring.)

Augur is the root of the Latin verb *inauguro*, from which our modern words *inaugurate* and *inauguration* are derived. *Inauguro* first meant to consult the birds, but later came to mean to install a government official by the ceremony of consulting the birds. Which probably explains why a new president often asks advice from the outgoing president—a lame duck.

The Plots Thicken

Where would history be without conspiracies, assassinations and cabals? When you think of conspiracy, you can almost hear the plotters' collective breathing as they whisper secret schemes to one another. This respiratory rapport is appropriate, for *conspirare*, the Latin root of *conspire*, literally means to breathe together, and many conspiracies are breath-taking in more ways than one.

The word *assassin* is also related to inhaling. Some historians say members of a murderous, eleventh-century Islamic sect smoked the intoxicating plant hashish to gain visions of the paradise they thought they'd attain if they died trying to slay an enemy; hence, they became known as *hashishi*, Arabic for *hashish-takers*. Soon *hashishi* crept stealthily into French and English as *assassin*. By extension, *assassin* came to mean a person who commits murder, especially the murder a prominent person.

Another word for a group of plotters or intriguers is *cabal*. Many people base their etymology of *cabal* on an "initial" assumption: it's an acronym derived from the last names of King Charles II's five most influential ministers: Clifford,

Arlington, Buckingham, Ashley and Lauderdale. (In fact, these are simply the first names of Scarlett O'Hara's husbands.)

But linguists have discovered that *cabal* comes from the Hebrew word *cabala*, a Jewish religious philosophy based on an esoteric interpretation of Hebrew scriptures. In the English word *cabal*, this notion of an esoteric or secret intrigue still survives, which is a lot more than you can say for most members of cabals.

High Crimes and Misty Meanings

Though legislators may occasionally throw rotten fruit at an official they're impeaching, the word *impeach* has nothing to do with fruit. Etymologically speaking, the most fitting image of impeachment would be a public official with his foot caught in a trap. For the English verb *impeach* ultimately derives from the Latin words *in* and *pedica* (in a snare or fetter). The Latin verb *impedicare* (to entangle) became the Anglo-French word *empecher* and eventually the Middle English word *empechen*, meaning to impede, accuse, hinder or criticize.

A legal sense of *empechen*—to accuse, bring charges against—was first recorded in 1384. Eventually, *impeach* took on a more specific meaning: Parliament's formal accusation of treason or other high crimes. Americans borrowed this legal procedure and the term to describe it from the British, though some rowdier, Brooklyn types preferred the phrase "Trow da bum out!"

The key fact to know about *impeach*, of course, is that it refers to a penultimate, not ultimate, act. It means to charge or accuse, not to convict or remove from office. Thus, a president may be impeached by the House of Representatives, but to be removed from office, he or she must be tried and convicted (by a two-thirds vote) in the Senate, and then given a wedgie by rowdy senators wearing funny hats.

Another derivative of the Latin *impedicare* is the little-used verb *peach*. To peach is to inform against someone. "Middle level bureaucrats cravenly peach on their bosses," the *National Observer* once observed. The verbs *impeach* and *peach* are both originally derived from the same Latin root (*impedicare*), but *peach* lost its *im*—and its popularity—along the way.

And, as for our good old noun *peach*, this word for the exotic Asian tree and its delicious fruit derives, via Middle English and Old French, from the Latin word *persicum*, meaning perjury, er, I mean . . . Persia, where the peach tree was first grown. *Persicum* is a shortening of *malum Persicum* (Persian apple).

Letters of the Law

Let's cop the origins of words for police officers. *Cop* itself is not, as the folk etymology has it, an acronym for *constable on patrol*. In fact, it's a shortening of *copper*, which means someone who seizes, catches. *Copper* comes from the old verb *cop*, meaning to take hold of or catch. This sense of *cop* survives in our expressions *cop an award* or *cop a plea*.

When you see a mounted police officer, you're getting the origin of *constable* straight from the horse's mouth. That's because the first constables watched over stables. *Constable* derives from the Latin *comes stabuli* (officer of the stable).

Sheriff is a combination of the old words *shire* and *reeve*. A shire was an old-fashioned version of a county in England, and a reeve was a local administrator appointed by Anglo-Saxon kings. The reeve who ruled over a shire was called a *shire-reeve*, and eventually "a royal pain in the neck."

You might wonder why the guys recruited by a sheriff to pursue the bad guy in westerns were called a *posse*. (You also might wonder why the same guys who had been hiding behind tables and beer kegs during the sheriff's gun fight with the villain were suddenly willing to risk their lives pursuing him.)

Posse is a shortening of the Latin phrase *posse comitatus*. *Posse* means body of men in Latin and comes from the Latin verb *posse* (to be able). (The implication is that this group of men was capable, potent.) *Comitatus* means county. So essentially a posse is a group of county employees on Viagra—eeek!

The word *police* itself comes from the Greek *polis* (city), while *flatfoot*, first appearing in the U.S. in 1913, refers to an officer's constant pounding of the pavement. Speaking of feet, a detective (a term shortened to *dick* by 1900) is called a *gumshoe* because he or she often sneaks around quietly in gum-soled shoes.

The phrase *good cop-bad cop* arose from a police interrogation method in which one officer assumes a harsh, hostile manner, while a second disarms the suspect with sympathy ("We know you didn't mean to kill her, Billy"). Today the phrase is often used to describe the contrasting roles played by two people working in tandem during meetings or negotiations.

As for the buzz on *fuzz*, well, the origins of this slang term are, appropriately enough, fuzzy.

Mudslingers

In case you hadn't noticed, politics is often mired in *libel, slander* and *scandal.*

If you carve a derogatory epithet on a tree, you may be accused of libel. That's appropriate, for the word *libel* comes from the Latin word for bark. The ancient Romans wrote most of their books on the inner bark of the papyrus plant, *liber* in Latin. Soon *liber* came to denote book, and *libellus*, a small book. Eventually *libellus* became *libelle* in French and *libel* in English.

By the 1500s, *libel* had come to denote the small book we now call a leaflet. Because these libels were often screeds denouncing prominent people, *libel* came to mean the publication of any harmful, defamatory statement.

Just as *libel* is rooted in bark, *slander* grew from another kind of wood—a stumbling block. The ancient Greek word *skandalon*, meaning a stumbling block or trap, became *scandalum* in Latin where it took on a metaphoric sense of something that causes sin.

Eventually, *scandalum* became *esclandre* in Old French, *slaundre* in Middle English, and *slander* in Modern English, where it now means the uttering of false and damaging claims against someone. (In today's legal use, *slander* refers to defamation by spoken words, and *libel* to defamation by written words.)

The Latin word *scandalum* also gives us the English *scandal*. While *scandal* originally referred only to the disgrace caused by stumbling into sin, we modern, nonjudgmental types now use *scandal* to refer only to earth-shattering, major offenses like pilfering cookies at the PTA bake sale.

MOTLEYS JUSTES

A Fascinating Assort-meant

This penultimate chapter provides a potpourri of intriguing word origins. You'll learn the origins of words associated with primal human preoccupations: love, money, danger—the whole ball of wax. Yeah, that's in there too.

Love Letters

How do I love thee? Let me count the words! The word *love* derives from the Old English *lufu*, which in turn comes from the Indo-European root *leubh* (to care, desire). Other love children of *leubh* are *belief* (a loved idea), *leave* (permission based on love, as in "I grant you leave"), and *libido* (love machine, à la Austin Powers).

English still carries a torch for the Greek and Latin words for love. Our language has *philandered* with the Greek hunk *phil*, as in *philosophy* (love of wisdom), *philanthropy* (love of human beings), *Grecophile* (love of Greece), and even *philodendron* (love of trees, because this plant often twines itself around tree trunks).

A long time ago, the Greek goddess of love, Aphrodite, slipped an *aphrodisiac* (food or drink that intensifies sexual desire) into English, leaving our language more vulnerable to her Roman counterpart, Venus, who gives us the respectable *venerate* (to love, respect) but also the disreputable *venereal* (transmitted by love, i.e., sexual contact).

Our love-starved language has also gone looking for love in all the young faces. English has fallen for Aphrodite's son

Eros, as in *erotic* and *erogenous*, and his Roman counterpart Cupid, as in *cupidity* and that arch little archer himself. Ay, there's the cherub!

What's more, the Latin word for love, *amor*, gives us *paramours* (lovers) who feel *amorous* (lovey-dovey) even if they're *amateurs* (people who pursue an endeavor out of sheer love, such as those who study eels for fun). Now that's a moray!

Let's affectionately grab some other love handles. *Fond*, for instance, reflects the fact that people in love sometimes act like fools. *Fond* comes from *fonned*, the past participle of the archaic verb *fonnen*, meaning to be foolish. So when Shakespeare's character Julius Caesar tells Metellus Cimber to "be not fond," he means, be not foolish (and stop fondling that knife under your toga).

And if you break bread every morning with a lover, he or she may become known as your *companion*. That's appropriate, because *companion* comes from the Late Latin *companio*, someone you break bread (*panis*) with (*com*).

Till Death Do Us Parse

From the moment a woman is "spoken for," words play a large role in weddings.

The word *wife* descends directly from *wif* (rhymes with *life*), the oldest English word for a woman. Eventually, *wif* was transformed to *wifeman*, then to *wimman* and finally to *woman*, and *wif* was left to denote a married woman only. For a while in Middle English, *wif* also meant a landlady or the mistress of a household, whether married or not, and this is where our word *midwife* originated. By the way, the male equivalent of *wif* was *wer* (man), a root that still howls in *werewolf* (man-wolf).

The word *bridal*, like some guests at a wedding reception, is filled with ale. *Ale* once meant festival, feast, so a *bridal* (*bryd ale*) was a wedding feast. Because the suffix *-ale* was mistaken for an adjectival *-al* ending (as in *natal*), *bridal* became a modifier (*bridal gown*).

Bridegroom was originally *bryd-guma*, *guma* meaning a man. But when people misheard *guma* as *groom*, it became *bridegroom*, a word lexicographer Noah Webster denounced because he felt it implied a husband groomed his bride as if she were a reliable steed.

Speaking of husbandry, *husband*, a combination of the old English word *hus* (house) and *bonde* (owner), originally meant the mistress of a house. Then, in an odd bit of linguistic gender bending, the men who married these house-owning women started to be called *husbands*, and the term *husband* eventually came to mean a married man.

Wedlock itself, happily, has nothing to do with a lock. It descends from the Old English *wedd* (pledge) and the suffix *-lac* (activity). Though at one time *wedlock* meant both a wedding and a wife, it now means the state of marriage.

Money Where Your Mouth Is

Money makes the world go 'round. And it also makes the words go 'round. Here's a cache of coinages for cash and coins.

Penny, a term we inherited from England, is derived from the Latin *pannus* (a piece of cloth) because fabric was once used as a medium of exchange. (And, no, this isn't a fabrication.) Throwing my two cents in, I'll tell you that *nickel* designated a three-cent piece until 1875, and the expression "Don't take any wooden nickels" first appeared about 1915. *Dime* (spelled *disme* on the first coins) is derived from the French *dixiéme*. In fact, though Americans were supposed to pronounce *dime* as *deem*, most deemed this pronunciation a dime-store Frenchification and ignored it.

A *bit*, meaning twelve and one-half·cents, first did its bit in English in 1688. It may be a translation of the Spanish *pieza* (piece), or may have come from the fact that early coins were literally bits and pieces of larger coins. The pirates' treasured *piece of eight*, for instance, was one-eighth of a Spanish *real*. If a rookie buccaneer expected praise for stealing just one piece of eight, his shipmates would tell him to "get real," and then cut his ear off and sell it for a buck.

Speaking of bucks, *dollar* is derived from *Joachimsthaler*, a coin first minted in the Czechoslovakian town of Joachimsthal in 1519. As *joachimsthalers* started spreading around Europe, they became known as *thalers*, *dalers*, and eventually *dollars*. Soon store clerks were asking customers, "Will you be paying by Czech or check?" The newly independent United States, tired of being "pounded" by Britain, established the dollar as its basic unit of paper money in 1792, and this term has retained its currency.

Here's a word origin that's truly on the money: A ten-dollar bill is called a *sawbuck* because the original bills were imprinted with the Roman numeral *X*, which reminded wood-cutting, wooden-nickel-taking Americans of a sawhorse or sawbuck. Because $10 bills issued by the Citizens' Bank of New Orleans were inscribed with the French word for ten (*dix*), they became known as *Dixies*, which is why, some etymologists believe, the entire South soon became known as *Dixie Land*. But others nix *dix* as *Dixie*'s source.

Finally, you ask, why do we call a dollar a *buck*? Because a buckskin was an early unit of trade in America. Now you know the "antler."

Jiving Dangerously

Let's play *Jeopardy!* Today's category is origins of words associated with danger.

Jeopardy itself derives from the French expression *jeu parti*, literally, "a game divided." In Old French, a *jeu parti* was an early version of our "he said, she said"—a poem, story or game that juxtaposed two opposed viewpoints. When Middle English borrowed *jeu parti* as *jeopardy*, this notion of a back-and-forth struggle in which either side could win or lose gave *jeopardy* the meaning of risk or peril. (Originally, a *jeopardy* meant a situation that could bring either success or failure, but human beings, inherent pessimists that they are, have emphasized the word's negative connotation.)

Hazard originally referred to a dice game. The story goes that it was invented during the Crusades to pass the time during the siege of a Palestinian castle called *Hazard* or *Azart*.

Crusader #1: How much longer can Hazard hold out?

Crusader #2: Dunno. Your roll.

Unfortunately, this theory is a bit dicey. For one thing, the name of the castle was actually *Ain Zarba*. For another, the Crusaders preferred playing poker.

But the French *hasard*, from which *hazard* is derived, probably does come from *as-zahr*, Arabic for the die, one of the dice. When *hazard* entered Medieval English, it meant the outcome of the roll of the dice and, eventually, any chance or venture. As with *jeopardy*, its meaning has since narrowed to refer only to obstacles, traps and other dangers.

When *danger* first appeared in Middle English as *daunger*, it meant not peril but power. *Daunger*, in fact, comes from the Latin *dominium*, ownership. So, when fourteenth-century English peasants spoke of someone's *daunger*, they meant his ownership, jurisdiction, dominion. And they soon discovered that anyone living within a *daunger* could be subjected to tyranny, injustice and violence.

Peasant #1: Whose daunger are you in?

Peasant #2: Lord Beats-his-serfs. How 'bout you?

Peasant #1: Lord Locks-'em-up.

And that's how *danger* came to mean jeopardy.

Waxing Eloquent

In the movie *Horsefeathers*, Groucho Marx plays a harried college president who receives this report from his secretary: "The Dean is furious. He's waxing wroth." Groucho replies, "Is Roth out there too? Tell Roth to wax the Dean for a while."

Like Groucho, you might find the phrase *wax wroth* confusing. One meaning of *wax* is to grow or become, as in "wax eloquent" or a "the moon is waxing" (perfect for nighttime cross-country skiing). *Wroth* is an adjectival form of *wrath*. So we speak of people who "wax indignant," "wax resentful" and, yes, when very angry, wax Roth himself (even though he devised a perfectly good IRA).

Back to *wax*. You might wonder why we refer to *the whole ball of wax*. Was it a spherical glob thrown by candlemakers who had waxed wroth? A huge, lavish dance at Madame Tussaud's?

Phrase detectives William and Mary Morris have traced this term to an archaic legal procedure, recorded in a 1620 text on English law. In order to divide up land among heirs of an estate, a description of each parcel of land was written on a scrap of paper. Then each scrap of paper was encased in a ball of wax, so no one could read the description.

Each heir would select a ball to determine which parcel he or she would inherit. That's how the entire estate—mansion, fields, vineyards, wax works, wax myrtle and yellow waxy buildup—became *the whole ball of wax*.

Some word historians claim wax may also play a role in the origin of *sincere*. Their story goes that unethical Roman stonemasons would sometimes coat the surface of marble with wax to give it a smooth and shiny appearance, thus bypassing the laborious process of polishing. In response, ethical stonemasons supposedly marketed their authentic polished marble as being *sine cera*, meaning without wax. Thus, *sincere* came to mean honest, genuine.

But lately this "marblelous" theory has been waning, not waxing. Most scholars now believe that *sincere* derives from the Latin *sincerus*, meaning whole, pure, authentic. *Sincerus*, they speculate, may have once meant one growth (not mixed), from *sin-* (one) and *crescere* (to grow). *Crescere* derives from *Ceres*, the goddess of grain, as in *cereal*. So the origins of *sincere* probably have more to do with Wheaties than wax.

Noodling on Caboodle

My dentist recently asked me about the origin of another term for *the whole ball of wax*—*the whole kit and caboodle*. And, when someone regularly pokes around in your mouth with a whole kit and caboodle of razor-sharp instruments, you don't let him down. He understands the *whole kit* part all right, a *kit* being that bag filled with useless items—such as a Timeshare Resort Condo Kit—that you throw into the garbage as soon as you receive it. You did throw that out, didn't you?

But what really intrigues him is *caboodle*, that silly-sounding word that seems slightly goofy, frivolous and, let's admit it—naughty. I mean, if I told you to "shake your caboodle," what would you do? (No phone calls, please.)

Most scholars believe the original form of this American phrase was "the whole kit and bilin'," *kit* meaning the whole thing, and *bilin'* (a corrupted form of *boiling*), meaning a seething mass, especially a seething mass of people. So *the whole kit and bilin'* meant the entire group of people and their equipment. (Why am I thinking of the ten guys who show up with two snowplows, three snowblowers and five snow shovels to clear my modest driveway?)

Anyway, along came throngs of Dutch immigrants to America. They arrived with their *boedel*, the Dutch word for household effects—wooden shoes, tulips, windmills, liberalized laws on drugs and euthanasia—the whole works. Soon American English adopted *boedel* as *boodle*, where it came to mean any collection of people, of illicitly obtained money or of stolen goods.

Before long, *boodle* had replaced *bilin'* in the phrase *the whole kit and bilin'*. Then, because human speech naturally favors alliteration, a *k* sound was prefixed to *boodle*, and *caboodle* was born.

But wait! That's not the whole kit and caboodle! In 1972, Ian Hancock, a Canadian linguist, suggested that *caboodle* derives, not from *boodle*, but from *kabudu*, a word in the Krio language of Sierra Leone. *Kabudu*, he speculated, may have entered American English through a Pidgin-Creole dialect of Louisiana.

So the true origin *of the whole kit and caboodle* is, as my dentist likes to say, open wide.

In a Predica-meant

If you're currently caught between the devil and the deep blue sea or a rock and a hard place, put this book down right now and make a decision! If not, keep reading and discover the unpredictable origins of some predicament phrases. You might call their stories "Wuthering Plights."

between Scylla and Charybdis—As the ancient Greek hero Odysseus and his men attempted to sail home from Troy, they were forced to navigate between two dangerous cliffs. (For this part of *The Odyssey* many high school students are tempted to rely on *Cliff's Notes*.) Guarding one promontory was the horrible monster Scylla whose six vicious dog heads were poised to strike. Near the other cliff lurked Charybdis whose voracious vortex waited to devour passing ships.

Faced with these two unpleasant alternatives (six of one and half a dozen whirlpools of the other), Odysseus made a tough choice. Rather than lose his entire ship to Charybdis, he risked a run past Scylla and lost six men to her canine jaws.

between a rock and a hard place—Some suggest that this contemporary expression evolved from Odysseus' cliffhanger. But others rock that boat, saying it came either from an idiom once used in Arizona to describe bankruptcy or from the Latin phrase *inter aram saxumque* (between an altar and a rock).

in a pickle—This expression is derived, not from the shriveled cucumber we call a *pickle*, but from the brine and vinegar in which it sits. Because this liquid is also called a *pickle*, anyone stuck in a tight spot is said to be *in a pickle*. This usage in English may have been influenced by the Netherlands phrase *in de pekel zitten* (sit in the pickle). So someone in a pickle may also be in Dutch.

QUIZZICAL EXPRESSIONS
Test Your Etymological IQ

his final chapter allows you to test your knowledge of word origins. It includes a variety of formats: multiple choice, true/false and short answer. Correct answers are provided at the end of the chapter. Watch out for trick questions!

Fish Stories

Which of these commonly accepted word origins are accurate?

1) A group of fish is called a *school* because fish swim together like kids in a school.

2) *Coward* is derived from *cow*, an animal that's easily frightened.

3) *Buckaroo*, meaning cowboy, refers to the bucking of a cowboy from his horse.

4) Our galaxy is called the *Milky Way* because its many stars make it look like milk.

5) A *quarry* is so called because stonecutters seek out rocks with the vigor of hunters pursuing their quarry.

6) The bird *cardinal* is so named because its red color resembles the color of a Catholic cardinal's robe.

7) *Infantry* is so called because it's composed of young (infant) soldiers.

8) *Hookers* are named for the large cadre of prostitutes who traveled with soldiers commanded by General Joseph Hooker during the Civil War. (You might say they were "tramping" out the vintage where the grapes of wrath are stored.)

Answers:

1) Nope. Anyone who has seen groups of school kids, as I do every day, knows fish are much more orderly in their travels. The fish type of school derives from the Old English *scolu*, meaning multitude. The education type of *school* comes from the Latin *schola*, meaning leisure devoted to learning.

2) "Udderly" ridiculous, though *coward* is derived from animal behavior. It comes from the Old French *coe* (tail) because a scared animal shows its tail as it flees.

3) Naaaay! *Buckaroo* is an American rendition of *vaquero*, the Spanish word for cowboy.

4) "Udderly" true! In fact, the ancient Greeks called the vast whiteness of stars *galaxis*, from *gala* (milk).

5) Sorry about *quarry*. A hunter's *quarry* comes from the French *cuiree*, the part of a slain animal's entrails fed to the hounds. A rock *quarry* is cut from the Old French *quarre* (squared stone).

6) You're well read! And each winter a college of cardinals gathers at your bird feeder.

7) You've come a long way, baby! Indeed, *infantry* marches into English from the Latin *infant*, meaning incapable of speech, young.

8) Forget that hoary legend. Attributing *hooker* to the Civil War would be a neat trick, because this term was walking the streets of American slang as early as 1845. *Hooker* may be derived from Corlear's Hook (a tawdry section of New York City) or the British term *hooker* (for petty thief). Others offer another angle: the similarity between soliciting men and hooking fish.

My Lips Are Sealed

Is there a linguistic connection between *seal*, meaning an aquatic mammal, and *seal*, meaning an emblem or a device for securing something? (Hmmmm . . . Well, when seals clap their front flippers together and grunt "uuh, uuh, uuh," might they be giving a seal of approval?)

Sorry. The animal *seal* comes from the old English *seolh*; the emblem or closure seal from the Middle English *seel*, from the Latin *sigillum*, small sign.

Now take this true/false quiz and see whether you know which sound-alike words actually share the same roots:

1) Both a money bank and a river bank are places where large quantities of something are piled up.

2) The verb *coast* (to glide) comes from traveling easily along the seacoast.

3) The rubbish *litter* comes from the stretcher *litter*.

4) The nobleman *count* is so called because he counts (enumerates) his subjects.

5) The *muscle* in your arm and the *mussel* you eat are derived from the same root.

Answers:

1) False. The money *bank* comes from the Old Italian *banca* (bench), the river *bank* from the Old Norse *bakki* (mound).

2) True. They both come from the Latin *costa* (rib, side). Originally, the verb *coast* meant to move along the seashore (where navigation is often easiest) or to skirt the side of something; later it became generalized to mean to move easily, glide.

3) True. Both words come from the French *lit* (bed). When the straw or hay in a litter was strewn about, it was also called litter, which soon came to describe any scattered rubbish.

4) False. The nobleman *count* comes from the Late Latin *comes*, *comit-* (companion), the enumeration *count* from the Latin *computere* (to calculate).

5) True. Both the body's *muscle* and the mollusk *mussel* are derived from the Latin *musculus* (little mouse). The Romans thought the muscles of the arms and legs looked like mice, with the tendons resembling tails. *Mussel* also comes from *musculus*, though it's not clear whether this creature was named for its resemblance to a human muscle or to a mouse.

Purple Prose

Does the color *maroon* have anything to do with being marooned on an island? Nice try. The color *maroon* derives from *marron*, the French word for the Spanish chestnut, which has a reddish-brown color. The abandoned *maroon* is derived from the Spanish *cimarrón* (wild, savage) and once referred to runaway slaves in the West Indies.

For more wild abandonment, take this true/false quiz:

1) *Clink*, the term for a jail, comes from the metallic sound made by the locks on cells.

2) A toady is said to *fawn* over someone because this posture resembles a doe ministering to her fawn.

3) The phrase *spruce up* has its roots in the spruce tree.

4) A musical *band* is so called because it's composed of strips or bands of musicians.

5) The cloth *canvas* and *canvass*, meaning to solicit support are woven of the same linguistic cloth.

Answers:

1) False. The term for a jail derives from the name of a prison in the London borough of Southwark. This jail, notorious for its miserable conditions, was named for a section of the Manor of Southwark called *Clink*.

2) False. The sycophant's *fawning* comes from the Old English *fagian* (to rejoice), the deer *fawn* from the Middle French *feon, faon* (young of an animal).

3) True. Prussia, once known as *Pruce* or *Spruce* in English, exported quality items known as *spruce iron, spruce trees* and *spruce leather*. Someone wearing a fashionable jacket made of spruce leather was said to be *spruce* or *spruced up*, and this became a general term for smartly attired.

4) False. *Band*, meaning strip or binding, derives from the Old Norse *band* (fetter), the musical *band* from the Middle French *bande* (troop).

5) True. Both come from the Latin *cannabis* (hemp). To *canvas* someone meant to toss him into a canvas sheet. By extension, *canvas* and its variant *canvass* came to mean to beat or buffet and to thrash out or discuss. It's likely this latter use

gave rise to the current meaning of *canvass*: to roam through an area soliciting political support or opinions.

Location Locutions

During the 1400s, some hard-working wagon makers in the small town of Kocs in northwest Hungary had a brilliant idea: Let's break for lunch. Over goulash, they had another brilliant idea: Let's build a wagon designed to carry passengers comfortably over bumpy, washed-out roads.

Their well-made carriages proved so popular that any similar vehicle became known as a *Kocs*, which rolled into German as *Kotsche*, into French as *coche* and into English as *coach*.

Coach is one of many words named for geographic locations. Can you match these other familiar words with the places they were born?

Words: 1) suede 2) canter 3) laconic 4) tabby

Places: a) suburb in Iraq b) region in Greece c) Scandinavian country d) town in England

1-c. The French thought soft, napped leather gloves from Sweden were the height of style. They called these gloves *gants de Suéde* (gloves of Sweden), and the shortened version of this phrase, *suede*, came to mean a type of leather with a soft napped surface.

2-d. The origins of *canter* lie in Canterbury in southeastern England, a popular destination for pilgrims such as those depicted in Geoffrey Chaucer's *Canterbury Tales*. A "gallop" poll taken at the time showed that 78.8 percent of these pilgrims rode to Canterbury on horses traveling at an easygoing, but swift pace known as the *Canterbury gallop* (plus or minus 3 percent margin of error). By the 1600s *Canterbury gallop* had been shortened to *Canterbury*, and by the 1700s to *canter*.

3-b. I'll be brief. Laconia was the region of ancient Greece where the Spartans lived, a people noted for their brevity in speech. For instance, when a warlord threatened, "If I come to Laconia, not one brick will stand on another," the Laconians sent a one-word reply: "If." It's no wonder that *laconic* came to mean terse or concise.

4-a. The cat is out of the Baghdad. The tabby, a domestic cat with a striped or brindled coat, still haunts the streets and alleys of al-'Attabiya, the Baghdad suburb for which it's named. In Medieval Latin *al-'Attabiya* became *attabi*; in French *tabis*; in English *tabby;* and, in the immortal words of my exasperated father during my sister's cat phase, "Where the heck did we get this moth-eaten thing?"

Take My Word for It

The English language is a great thief. Each of the following sentences, for instance, contains several words stolen from another language. Can you tell which language provided the words for each sentence? (Look for the hidden clue in each sentence.)

1) I wouldn't choose to cruise by a bluff where a boss, a snoop and a bully loitered.

2) Here's my saga: I got the mumps near a geyser on the rocks.

3) Near a cairn made of fake stones were crags and bogs galore.

4) Check your howitzers, pistols and robots at the door.

5) Amidst the flummery about cetaceans were stories of corgis, bugs and penguins dressed in flannel.

6) In the bungalow next to the new deli, pundits and gurus in dungarees and pajamas make a lot of loot selling shampoo.

7) On a rainy plain, near a ranch with a barricade and a silo, a vigilante tossed a grenade at a cask and started a stampede.

8) The great Wall Street tycoon, refusing to kowtow to gung-ho guys, put ketchup on her kumquat and kaolin in her tea.

Answers:

1) Dutch: cruise, bluff, boss, snoop, bully, loiter ("wouldn't choose"—wooden shoes)

2) Icelandic: saga, mumps, geyser ("on the rocks"—ice)

3) Gaelic: cairn, crag, bog, galore ("fake stones"—shamrocks)

4) Czech: howitzer, pistol, robot ("Check"—Czech)

5) Welsh: flummery, corgi, bug, penguin, flannel ("cetaceans"—whales, Wales)

6) Indian (Hindi/Urdu): bungalow, pundit, guru, dungarees, pajamas, loot, shampoo ("new deli"—New Delhi)

7) Spanish: ranch, barricade, silo, vigilante, grenade, cask, stampede ("rainy plain"—"the rain in Spain" from *My Fair Lady*)

8) Chinese: tycoon, kowtow, gung-ho, ketchup, kumquat, kaolin, tea (great Wall—Great Wall)

Godspell

Pallas Athena, the Greek goddess of wisdom and the arts, inspired two grand English words: *athenaeum* (also spelled *atheneum*) and *palladium*. *Athenaeum* means an institution for the promotion of learning or a repository of books or art, such as the Wadsworth Atheneum, an art museum in Hartford, Connecticut. As for *palladium*, the Trojans believed that a sacred statue of Athena, called the *palladium* after *Pallas*, protected their city from invasion.

So the English word *palladium* means an object or tradition that guards a nation or way of life. The film ratings system, for instance, could be described as a "the palladium of American decency"—or maybe not. (Speaking of movies . . . somehow English speakers also came to associate *palladium* with an ancient circus or theater, hence this word's occasional use for a majestic movie house.)

Athena is only one of many gods and goddesses from Greek mythology whose names flourish in English words. Can you match these deities with their names and English words derived from them?

Gods and goddesses:

1) goddess of the Earth

2) a sea god who could change his shape

3) god of the sun

4) goddess of the dawn
5) god of death
6) god of sleep
7) goddess of darkness
8) god of the underworld
9) goddess of love
10) goddess of rainbows

Names and words:

a) Eos—*Eocene* (first part of the Cenozoic period in geologic history, "dawn of the new")

b) Nox—*nocturnal* (related to night)

c) Helios—*helium* (an element so named because scientists mistakenly thought it existed only on the sun)

d) Proteus—*protean* (having a varied nature or the ability to assume different forms)

e) Iris—*iris* (colored part of the eye); *iridescent* (rainbow-like)

f) Pluto—*plutocrat* (wealthy, because rich metals come from beneath the ground)

g) Hypnos—*hypnosis* (a sleep-like state)

h) Gaia—*geography, geology, geometry* (measurement of the Earth)

i) Aphrodite—goddess of love (*aphrodisiac*—food or drink that arouses desire)

j) Thanatos—*thanatology* (the study of the phenomenon of death)

Answers:

1-h; 2-d; 3-c; 4-a; 5-j; 6-g; 7-b; 8-f; 9-i; 10-e

Index

Index